# GOING DOWN STICKY TOFFEE LANE

Recipes & Stories from

Chef George Fowler

Printed and bound in Turkey
First Printing, 2015

ISBN 978-0-9931605-0-9

Published by Chef George Fowler
PO Box 30319
Grand Cayman  KY1-1202, Cayman Islands

www.StickyToffeeLane.com

I'd like to dedicate this book to my sister, Jean, for her inspiration.

# My Thanks

To Lynda Granlien and Preston Randall, without whom we would not have a book!
To my good friends Stephen and Wanda Trench, Len Eastwood,
James Mason, Teresa Grimes and Lisa Macaulay, all of whom were a great help to me.
To Paul Furze, my Sous-Chef and all the staff at Calypso Grill — front and back of house.
I am very grateful to Ergun and Petra Berksoy — a big thank you.
Thanks also to Sarah Cremese, Shelley Leonard, Philip Kirham and
Marilyn Gould for help with the photos.
My special gratitude to John Davis for the front cover photo of me.
And to Michael and Jean Pearson who were there for me at the beginning
of my journey down Sticky Toffee Lane.

# CONTENTS

## Mains

## Desserts

## Extras

# Introduction

When I was young I always had a robust appetite — I liked good food. However, all food was certainly at a premium; times were hard and there was rationing in England. But one thing was still guaranteed in my young life, and that was my Sunday visit to Grandma on when she would cook for our entire family. She would make traditional savoury dishes and sweet treats alike and her warm, welcoming home and kitchen was my introduction to comfort, love and fulfilment. As I got older I learned I could create dishes, too, and share the way I felt about food with other people. So I've spent over forty years doing just that; trying to create excellent, flavourful food that will make a memorable experience for my diners, my guests, my friends and family. Of course I did the prerequisite French culinary training in the Escoffier method of cooking when I was young. I started when I was 15 years old and have worked perfecting my skills as a chef ever since. Along the way I met some very colourful people and I've enjoyed living in many different countries, islands and cultures. I hope you enjoy my stories and recipes — they were written especially for you! And please, by all means, when you're in Grand Cayman stop by Calypso Grill and ask for me, Chef George — I'm always happy to talk.

# Foreword
## by Chef Eric Ripert

"Going Down Sticky Toffee Lane" is a great homage to George Fowler, the iconic Calypso Grill, and Grand Cayman. When visiting the island, I always make sure to find the time to stop by Calypso Grill for a visit. I love the energy of the room, being surrounded by the beautiful ocean views and, of course, the delicious food.

I have wonderful memories of time spent with friends, indulging in great meals and great wine — all of which inspire a strong connection to the Caribbean, its fresh ingredients, and warm traditions.

This book, filled with beautiful photos, short stories, and delicious recipes, brings back those happy memories and will have a special place in my heart and on my book shelf at home.

# Grandma's

I suppose this is the beginning of my journey down Sticky Toffee Lane. Growing up I did not do a lot of cooking at home but that does not mean I wasn't interested! I remember spending every summer vacation at my grandma's at Burnhope, a lovely town on a hill in Durham, and being very excited as she always made ginger snaps for me. Her kitchen was in the sitting room where the fire and oven were side-by-side. It was not a commercial oven, you see, and my grandma actually controlled the temperature by packing the coals on the fire in a very particular way.

And every Sunday throughout the year our big family of about twenty would descend upon Grandma's house and she typically would prepare a leg of pork, stuffing with sage, mashed potatoes, mushy peas, and whatever vegetables were available from the fruit man who came by her door each week (and she always served at least six vegetables.)

It was magical to me that she cooked all the dishes for all the meals with pans and pots put directly onto the fire while the baking was done in the oven. When all the food was cooked, the pies, biscuits, stews and all would be on the hearth in front of the fire to keep warm. As a young lad, those visits to my grandma's were happy times for me. The wonderful smells and appearance of my grandma's cooking are firmly imprinted in my mind to this day.

# ARUGULA SALAD
# WITH FETA, BEETROOT & SQUASH

## INGREDIENTS

1 lb beetroot
1 lb butternut squash
Salt & pepper
Olive oil
8 oz arugula, pre-washed
½ cup Calypso House Salad Dressing (recipe page 133)
4 oz feta cheese

## METHOD

**Boil** the beetroot in a large pan making sure it is well covered at all times. Cook for approximately 30 minutes. Keep testing with a skewer or sharp knife, until it comes out easily. When cooked and cooled, peel the beetroot and dice into ½-inch cubes.

**Peel** and seed the butternut squash and dice into ½-inch cubes. Place onto a roasting tray and sprinkle with salt and pepper, and toss with a touch of olive oil – enough to coat the squash. Bake at **350°F** for approximately 15 minutes.

**To assemble** the salad, place the arugula into the bowl with the beetroot and the roasted butternut squash. Add the dressing and toss the salad really well. Divide onto 4 plates and crumble the feta on top. Serve.

**Serves 4.**

*Seed the butternut squash easily with a large spoon.*
*When peeling the beetroot it's a good idea to use plastic gloves as it dyes your hands red.*
*When placing the cheese on the salad, it can be crumbled or diced into small cubes. It is a good idea to buy a high quality feta cheese.*

# GREEK SALAD

## INGREDIENTS

2 limes
½ cup olive oil
1 tbsp dried oregano
2 lb tomatoes, diced ½-inch
1 whole cucumber, seeded and diced ½-inch
½ cup Kalamata olives
1 green pepper, diced ½-inch
1 small onion, diced ½-inch
8 oz feta cheese

## METHOD

**To assemble** the salad: squeeze the limes in a bowl and add the olive oil. Mix in the oregano.
**Add** the tomatoes, cucumber, olives, green pepper and onion. Stir to cover the vegetables. Marinate in the fridge for 2 hours.
**Crumble** the feta cheese onto the salad and mix well. Leave in the fridge until serving. Season to taste.
**Serves 6-8.**

*Use the best quality of feta cheese as it makes a great difference. Only use the ripest tomatoes for this dish as it's important that the tomatoes taste sweet. The tomatoes are what makes the salad.*

*It is a good idea to make the salad in the morning if it's for dinner as the longer the salad marinates, the better it tastes.*

*The ingredients I give you are a guide, especially for the dressing. It might need more lime, or less. Keep tasting the dressing until you are satisfied.*

*I always feel the need to use kosher salt for the tomatoes, which helps to sweeten them even more.*

# CALYPSO HOUSE SALAD

## INGREDIENTS

1 bunch fresh asparagus
½ cup Picholine olives, not pitted
1 cup canned chickpeas, rinsed and drained
½ cup Calypso House Salad Dressing (see recipe page 133)
2 romaine lettuce hearts
2 oz Parmesan, coarsely grated

## METHOD

**Place** the dressing in the bottom of a large bowl.
**Blanche** the asparagus in boiling salted water for 4 minutes. Take out and plunge into iced water. When cold, cut into approximately ½-inch pieces.
**Mix** the asparagus, olives and chickpeas into the dressing.
**Wash** the romaine lettuce and discard the outer leaves. Dry the lettuce and cut into ½-inch strips and add to the dressing. Toss all together in the bowl.
**Top** with Parmesan cheese and serve.
**Serves 4.**

*Adding all the ingredients to the dressing first, and just piling the lettuce on top, will marinate the vegetables nicely and allow you to prepare this salad ahead of time. Leave it in the fridge and toss the lettuce with the vegetables only when you are ready to serve.*

*I sometimes substitute mixed lettuce greens for one of the romaine hearts.*

*Pre-grated Parmesan is not a good substitute for Parmesan cheese bought in a block.*

# WARM GOATS' CHEESE SALAD

## INGREDIENTS

8 oz goats' cheese
¼ cup olive oil
1 tsp fresh Basil
1 tsp fresh oregano
Calypso House Salad (see recipe page 17)
2 cups fine breadcrumbs

## METHOD

**Cut** the cheese with a cheese wire into 4 equal slices. Mix the olive oil and fresh herbs on a flat dish. Marinate the cheese slices overnight, covered, in the refrigerator.

**Make** the Calypso House Salad as per recipe. Toss the salad only when ready to serve.

**Place** each slice of goats' cheese into the breadcrumbs and coat completely. Place the slices onto a baking tray and into a preheated oven at **350°F** for approximately 5 minutes – just long enough to warm the goat's cheese.

**Toss** the salad and place equally on 4 plates. Place each piece of goat's cheese on top of a salad and serve.

**Serves 4.**

*In order to cover the cheese slices evenly, be sure to start with plenty of breadcrumbs.*

*At the restaurant I use one of the best goats' cheeses on the market called Laura Chenel's Chèvre from Sonoma County in California. I am sure all the top chefs use this goats' cheese. If you happen to see it, it's well worth buying.*

*Tomatoes and/or fennel make nice additions to this salad.*

*I suggest you serve this salad with a nice crusty French loaf.*

# Imperial Hotel
## The First Step

My first port of call in the kitchen was at the Imperial Hotel in the market town of Darlington, county Durham. I needed some money to go down to London on a school trip so I went to the hotel's back door and asked if I could see the chef. Luckily, the second chef took me into the kitchen where I met the head chef; as I was only sixteen at the time, he seemed ancient!

I asked if he had any jobs in the kitchen helping out, and he told me there was plenty of work but no money to pay me. If I was interested I could start working weekends to see if I enjoyed it.

In spite of the lack of pay I was still very interested to see what it would be like and so I agreed and thanked him for the opportunity.

I'll never forget my first day. I was frightened out of my wits as I was shown around the huge kitchen and introduced to all the staff. The main thing I discovered that day was to be careful around the chef who had a seriously bad temper. To make things even worse, he wore bedroom slippers in the kitchen so you could never hear him coming. His nickname was "Slasher" — obviously not a name we used to his face.

I started doing menial tasks like peeling potatoes, carrots, and the like but the most "interesting" part was working with the chef himself. One day he needed some Worcestershire sauce from the storeroom which was a considerable distance from the kitchen and always kept locked. After a long walk and extensive search, though, I couldn't find any sauce and nervously returned to tell the chef there was none left. He proceeded to bellow at me and took my shaking hand all the way back to the storeroom where he immediately pulled some off the shelf saying, "We don't have any? Right, what's this?"

I knew I had seen that bottle when I was looking but all I saw was Lea & Perrins (which, of course, is the company that makes Worcestershire sauce). I never made that mistake again!

On another occasion I was cutting up onions on the opposite side of the table to Slasher while he cut some meat. Suddenly, with no warning, a huge knife sailed past my ear and stuck into the steel door of the fridge behind me! As I stood frozen to the spot in shock he started shouting about how dull his knife was. Over time I learned this wasn't unusual behaviour amongst chefs.

I also learned Chef's bark was worse than his bite. He was really an old softie — when I told him I was going to London the next weekend with the school he gave me some spending money out of his own pocket.

Although I never ended up working at the Imperial on a full-time basis I now look back on my experiences there with great fondness. After all, it was a great first step which started my future career as a chef and led to all the wonderful places in which I have lived and worked since then.

# CONCH CHOWDER

## INGREDIENTS

1 tsp olive oil

1 lg onion, finely chopped

1 lb carrots, diced ¼-inch

4 sticks celery, diced ¼-inch

1 med red pepper, diced ¼-inch

1 med green pepper, diced ¼-inch

2 cloves garlic, chopped

5 pieces conch meat, minced

½ lb tomatoes, chopped

1 tbsp tomato paste

4 cups vegetable stock

1 cup white wine

Salt to taste

1 fresh Scotch Bonnet pepper, seeded (optional)

## METHOD

**Sauté** the onion, carrots, celery, red and green peppers, garlic and conch meat in the olive oil. Sauté until the conch breaks up and then add the chopped tomatoes and tomato paste. Continue to sauté for 1 minute more then add the vegetable stock and white wine.

**Bring** to the boil and skim the soup. Simmer for 30 minutes, skimming whenever needed. Season to taste with salt. Serve.

**Serves 4-6.**

*Conch can be quite tough and inedible unless it's pounded or minced. For this recipe, conch is either minced by hand or by food processor. This breaks the muscle down and makes it more tender.*

*When simmering the soup, continue to skim, otherwise it could be bitter to taste.*

*Add a whole Scotch Bonnet when cooking if you'd like a bit of a kick.*

*Creamy chowder could be made by omitting the tomatoes and tomato paste and adding cream or coconut milk instead.*

# LOCAL BREADFRUIT CHOWDER

## INGREDIENTS

1 lg ripe breadfruit, peeled and diced 1-inch
Kosher salt to taste
2-3 tsp olive oil
1 lg onion, roughly chopped
2 cloves garlic
4 cups chicken stock
½ cup heavy cream
¼ cup butter
½ lb carrots, peeled and diced ¼-inch
4 sticks celery, diced ¼-inch
1 sm green pepper, seeded and diced ¼-inch
1 sm red pepper, seeded and diced ¼-inch

## METHOD

**Place** the diced breadfruit on a roasting tray and sprinkle with salt and about 1 tsp of the olive oil – just enough to stop it sticking to the pan. Roast at **350°F** for approximately 10-15 minutes or until just soft to the touch.

**Sauté** the onion and garlic in 1 tsp of the olive oil in a large pot. Add the roasted breadfruit and chicken stock. Bring to the boil then simmer for 10 minutes and then blitz the soup with an immersion blender. Add the cream and check the seasoning.

**Sauté** the diced vegetables in the butter for approximately 5 minutes over a moderate heat or until soft. Add to the soup and serve.

**Serves 4-6.**

*It's very important that the breadfruit is ripe to the touch but not too soft.*

*Vegetable stock instead of chicken stock is optional.*

# Devonport Hotel
## Middleton-One-Row, near Darlington

My first real paying job was as a trainee chef at the Devonport Hotel in Darlington. I was, in a way, lucky to get the job and I still believe to this day my father, who had already passed, was with me that day.

My first stroke of luck was that I was interviewed by the general manager and not the chef, Michael, who immediately pointed out if he had interviewed me I would not be there at all! He then put me "on trial" for one week, which I fortunately survived.

He was very tough on me and the older lad, Tony, who worked with us. Tony had been there a year so he was well-seasoned and, the truth of the matter was, the two of them ganged up on me and played pranks all day. Needless to say I was very conscientious and believed everything they said and told me to do.

In spite of the mischief, it was a great introduction to kitchen work and what lay ahead. Every Sunday afternoon, after lunch, the kitchen was stripped bare and we had to scrub every crook and cranny until it was gleaming. And because I was the youngest and newest I was given the hardest work. Thank God the restaurant was closed on Sunday evenings so I could recover!

One day per week I went to college for my City & Guild First Certificate and worked at the restaurant the other 5½ days. I really had hardly any time to myself and before I knew it two years had passed and I felt it was time to move to greener pastures. As you'll see in my other stories, some pastures turned out to be greener than others.

By the way, Tony eventually became very successful. I visited him at the Mayfair Hotel in London some twenty years later where he was the food and beverage manager. It was a delight to meet up with him again and see the amazing transformation from a cheeky, skinny kid in Darlington all those years ago to a confident, successful manager at a high-end London hotel.

Michael, the chef at the Devonport all those years ago, and his wife Jean are very good friends of mine to this day. They live in Australia where he continues to introduce naive new recruits into the restaurant business.

# ROASTED PUMPKIN SOUP

## INGREDIENTS

1 med pumpkin, peeled, seeded and diced 1-inch
2 tsp olive oil
1 large onion, peeled and diced
4 cups chicken stock
1 cup white wine
Salt and pepper to taste

## METHOD

**Place** the diced pumpkin on a roasting tray and lightly coat with the olive oil. Roast in the oven at **350°F** until the pumpkin starts to colour – approximately 10-15 minutes.
**In** a large pot, sauté the onions in a touch of olive oil without colouring them.
**Add** the pumpkin, chicken stock and white wine. Bring to the boil then simmer for about 10 minutes. Blitz the soup with an immersion blender. Season to taste and serve.
**Serves 4.**

*It's not necessary to roast the pumpkin, but it certainly makes a difference to the flavour.*

*If desired, a drop of heavy cream may be added prior to serving.*

*Roasted pumpkin seeds served atop the soup give it style!*

*An immersion blender is available in any hardware store. The are quite inexpensive, but they do wear out. I consider it an essential piece of equipment for my kitchen.*

# TOMATO & BASIL SOUP

## INGREDIENTS

1 tbsp olive oil
1 large onion, diced small
2 garlic cloves, minced
2 lb plum tomatoes, chopped
1 tsp tomato paste
8 leaves fresh basil
4 cups vegetable stock
A touch of heavy cream (optional)

## METHOD

**Heat** the olive oil in a sauté pan, add the onion and garlic and sauté for approximately 2 minutes over medium heat until the onions are translucent.

**Add** the tomatoes, tomato paste and basil and sauté for 5 more minutes.

**Add** the vegetable stock, bring to the boil, then simmer for about 5 minutes. Skim off any foam that forms on the surface. Blitz the soup with an immersion blender and bring back to the boil. Season to taste, adding a little sugar if it tastes acidic, but remember it's not a dessert. Add the touch of cream if desired, but personally, it's good without.

**Serves 4.**

*Using plum tomatoes is not essential. The best tomatoes to use are the freshest and the sweetest.*
*Tomato paste or puree is very good, but as in any dish, it has a strong flavour and should be used sparingly.*
*As an option, you may want to put a tsp of crème fraiche on the top of each bowl before serving.*

# CALYPSO SHRIMP

## INGREDIENTS

¼ cup butter
6 green onions, ¼-inch diced
1 tsp fresh ginger, peeled and finely grated
16 (16-20) shrimp, peeled and deveined
¼ cup white wine
1 cup Lemon Butter Sauce (see recipe page 136)
1 lb fresh baby spinach
½ Scotch Bonnet pepper, seeded and finely diced

## METHOD

**Place** butter into a large sauté pan with green onions, ginger and Scotch Bonnet and sauté until soft.

**Add** the shrimp and continue cooking until the shrimp are translucent. Add the wine and the Lemon Butter Sauce and bring to the boil. At this stage, remove the shrimp and keep warm.

**Reduce** the sauce until it coats the back of a spoon. Place the shrimp back into the pan and warm the shrimp slightly.

**Bring** 1 cup of salted water to the boil and place the spinach into the pot and cook just until wilted. Strain into a colander and drain well until all the water leaves the spinach.

**Divide** the spinach equally onto 4 plates. Top with shrimp and the sauce. Serve.

**Serves 4.**

*Use large shrimp for this recipe as any smaller and you will lose the taste of the dish.*

*Don't overcook the shrimp – they should be just firm to the touch. Overcooking shrimp causes them to be hard and unappetising.*

*The spinach will take only 1 minute to cook. Strain right away and serve. It's good to cook the spinach at the end so it stays green. Spinach colour can change very quickly. If you need to cook it earlier, place it into iced water after cooking and then strain. Heat the spinach again in a little butter in a sauté pan. You don't need a lot of sauce for this dish, just enough to coat the shrimp.*

# Fishermans Arms

## near Ulverston, the Lake District

It wasn't easy for me to find another job at home in Darlington but luckily Michael, my chef at the Devonport Hotel, offered me a job not far away at the Fishermans Arms in Baycliff — a small village near Ulverston in the Lake District. The small hotel overlooked Morcombe Bay but was still quite a distance from the bay itself. All the same it had a great water view of the Kent Channel. Once again I worked as a trainee chef under Michael — the difference being that Jeannie, his wife, worked there also, which I loved.

Just like at the Devonport, Michael cracked the whip and continued the Sunday "Deathly Cleaning Ritual."

Mr Dick Coyne was the owner and manager of the Fishermans Arms. He was a well-respected man in Lancashire as he was the president of the United Kingdom Bartenders' Guild. This was quite an honour and so he had plenty of connections in the catering industry. He was great fun — always laughing and joking with everyone.

One of the sons of the famous Moet & Chandon family, and a friend of the owner, came as a guest to the hotel on his honeymoon. As always Sunday evening was the quiet time of the week so the kitchen was closed. But I was asked to work that night regardless in case this "French VIP" needed something to eat in his room. As a young

trainee I was frightened to death and sat quivering in the kitchen for an hour.

Just as I started to think I wasn't needed, a head popped through the door saying, "I have a lovely English Rose who is peckish upstairs so could you please prepare two nice plain omelettes with a green salad." The food must have been okay because he came to see me every day thereafter and asked me to cook different meals for the two of them. I really felt quite honoured.

He left with his English Rose early one morning so unfortunately I did not get to say goodbye. Feeling sad, I went down to the kitchen where I discovered a case of Moet & Chandon with a note saying, "Thank you, Chef George." At the time it felt like a million dollars. Mr Coyne offered to buy them from me as he knew I needed the money more than the champagne. How true!

On another occasion Mr Coyne decided to have a party to celebrate his wedding anniversary. Chef Michael put us on alert that this was to be the best dinner party ever which meant long hours in the kitchen. We didn't mind so much, though, as everyone respected and liked Mr and Mrs Coyne a great deal. King Beef Wellington was on the menu and, as there were many courses, it was kept in the oven to coordinate the time of serving. The reason for this is that the beef will carry on cooking in the pastry if not carved and served after resting for five minutes.

Just as were ready to carve and serve the Wellington Mr Coyne declared, "Stop the main course!" Then he said to all the men at the table, "Let's go to the local pub for a beer." Mrs Coyne was not at all amused and Chef Michael even less so.

The pub, located just up the back lane from the hotel, was one of the oldest in Britain. In fact it wasn't a pub as we know them but a small cottage where you sat in the sitting room with a roaring fire. An old couple would ask what beer you preferred and fetch it from the tap room out back. It was a great place and very unique but they had to be quick as the place went crazy with our large group. However, at the end of the evening everyone considered it a great success — even Mrs Coyne.

One of the persons at the dinner party, Jack Neighbour, became very important to my career. Some time later, after I started at the Midland Hotel in Manchester, Mr Coyne told me to go to Hollins College and said Jack Neighbour would look after me as he was the head chef. When I went to the administration office to enrol they told me the college was full and I would have to attend at the neighbouring college in Salford.

The next day I rang Mr Coyne to say I wasn't able to get in. He told me rubbish! — of course I could go there. He asked me if I had spoken to Jack Neighbour and I confessed I had not. He told me to go back the next day.

When I returned to the college instead of going to the office I asked if I could speak directly with Jack Neighbour. This time she replied, "Yes, he's expecting you." To my astonishment and relief I was welcomed with open arms and I eventually trained under him for five years.

# CEVICHE

## INGREDIENTS

8 oz fresh wahoo or mahimahi, diced ½-inch
Kosher salt
1 cup white vinegar
1 small onion, diced ¼-inch
1 small mango, peeled, seeded and diced ¼-inch
3 tomatoes, seeded and diced ¼-inch
3 limes, juice and zest
1 orange, juice and zest
¼ cup fresh cilantro, chopped

## METHOD

**Season** the fish with salt. Add the white vinegar and refrigerate at least 2 hours.

**In** a bowl, gently mix together the onion, mango, tomato, fruit juices, zests and cilantro.

**Drain** the fish from the vinegar and add the fish to the mix. Refrigerate until ready to eat. Serve in 4 bowls.

**Serves 4.**

*Use fresh fish only, as this dish will be enhanced with the freshness.*

*Use only white distilled vinegar as this will help to firm the fish and, by leaving the fish in the fridge for at least 2 hours, the vinegar will help to cook the fish slightly.*

*When zesting the fruit be careful to take only the outside of the peel and not the bitter white underneath.*

# CRABCAKES

## INGREDIENTS

1 red pepper, seeded, finely diced
1 small onion, finely diced
2 sticks celery, finely diced
1 tbsp Worcestershire sauce
½ cup Hellmann's mayonnaise
1 tbsp Dijon mustard
1 egg
1 lb jumbo crab meat, fresh or canned
½ cup bread crumbs or Panko
1 oz cooking oil

## METHOD

**Place** red peppers, onion, and celery in a bowl with the Worcestershire sauce, mayonnaise, mustard and egg. Mix together well.

**Gently** fold in the crab meat and bread crumbs so the crab meat is not broken up too much.

**Form** the mixture into 8 crabcakes of equal portions, approximately 1½ oz each.

**Place** a pan onto the stove with the cooking oil and bring it to a moderate heat. Place your crabcakes into the pan until brown on one side then gently turn the crabcakes over and brown the other side. Cook for about 4 minutes per side.

**Serves 4** with lemon wedges as a starter or with Calypso House Salad (see recipe page 17) for lunch.

*I have found only the best quality of crab meat should be used for the best results. Large jumbo meat is the best. When mixing, be very careful not to break the crab too much or it will turn into mush. Also, when forming the cakes be very gentle, as they need to be a little loose when you cook them.*

*Excellent!*

# DUCK CONFIT

## INGREDIENTS

4 (6 oz) duck legs
Sea salt
1 lb jar duck fat
2 bay leaves
8 whole black peppercorns
1 lb small red bliss potatoes, halved and parboiled
4 cups baby mixed leafy greens
½ cup Cumberland Sauce (see recipe page 135)

## METHOD

**Remove** the small bone from the duck legs and just leave in the thigh bone. Liberally season the duck legs with sea salt. Wrap in plastic wrap and leave in the fridge overnight.
**Rinse** the duck legs under cold water and pat dry. Place the duck legs, bay leaves and peppercorns in an oven-proof roasting pan or dish. Melt the duck fat and pour over the legs to cover them. Cover with tin foil and bake at **250°F** for about 3 hours. At this stage, the legs should be soft. If you do not need them right away, leave them in the fat – the fat preserves the legs and they can be kept for a week like this in the refrigerator.
**When** you are ready to serve the duck legs, heat 3 tbsp duck fat in a hot skillet or frying pan and seal both sides of the legs. Add the parboiled potatoes and bake in the oven for 10 minutes at **400°F.** This will crisp the duck legs and roast the potatoes.
**Prepare** 4 plates with 1 cup mixed leafy greens then add 2 tbsp of Cumberland Sauce and place the leg on top of the sauce. Arrange the roast potatoes around the leg and serve.
**Serves 4.**

*If you buy the duck legs from a local butcher or supermarket you can ask him to take the thigh bone out for you. It's important to only have one bone in the duck leg as it will crisp better and will also be easier to eat.*

*The potatoes do not need to be red bliss. Any small kind of potato is fine. Parboil them for 5 minutes and then strain the water away – this helps to crisp the potatoes in the duck fat and finish cooking at the same time as the duck.*

*You can purchase jars of duck fat at the supermarket. The fat that is left over from cooking the duck can be placed back into the jar to use another time.*

*The sweet sauce of red currant jelly and port wine compliments the duck very well and the addition to a mixed leaf lettuce makes this a great dish.*

# The Midland Hotel
## Manchester, England

At age seventeen I was working in a small hotel in the Lake District. It was a great little place called The Fishermans Arms in Baycliffe overlooking Morcombe Bay where the shrimp are used for making that great dish Potted Shrimp. It's a shame I can't make them in Calypso but, unfortunately, we're not close enough to Morcombe Bay.

Getting back to the story, the owner of the hotel thought it was time for me to get some serious training and he suggested the Midland Hotel in Manchester. His nephew was a manager there and knew Monsieur Le Fèvre, the chef de cuisine, very well. So I went to the Midland Hotel to train to be a chef.

The hotel was built in Victorian times and when you went through the back door it was like walking into a massive rabbit burrow. Numerous changing rooms, the laundry and the bakery all led from the back entrance and it was quite easy to get lost. The huge kitchen was up a flight of stairs and included two levels. On one level was the Monkey Cage (more on that later) and on the other were the walk-in fridges and freezers. A butcher, buffet chef and everything that was served cold came from that area. There were over 60 cooks total in the kitchen. The cooks were of all levels and some were quite scary as I was the "new meat". In terms of the view, there were windows above but you could only see the feet of people as they walked past. This kitchen was also Victorian design at its best. "Upstairs, Downstairs" had nothing on this place; it was to be my home for four to five years and many happy days were spent there.

Anyway, I'm sure you're wondering what the Monkey Cage was. Well, it was a place where all the veg were kept and if you needed anything you had to ask the sous chef for the keys. The trainee chefs, including myself, were always playing pranks on each other and one day when I was in the Monkey Cage I heard the door slam behind me. The buggers had locked the cage behind me and run back to the kitchen with the keys. I thought it quite funny at first and shouted to tell them the joke was over. Then who should walk up the stairs but Monsieur Le Fèvre himself — the Big Chef, and here I was standing behind this wire mesh shouting my head off. "Ahhhhh, Mr Fooler, you fool me," he said, as this was his name for me — Mr Fooler not Fowler. I replied, "No Chef, they locked me in." He took one long look at me, shook his head and said, "I hope someone lets you out." Then he just walked away. I was shaking pretty good by that time as there was one thing you soon learnt it was, "Do NOT upset The Chef."

At that moment the sous chef came around the corner with the keys to let me out. "What the hell are you doing?

Stop messing around and get back to work — and by the way, keep out of Chef's sight as he will be after you and you are lucky that he is leaving soon."

I was worried sick all morning and finally after some time the chef approached, grabbed my ear and twisted it. "Somebody has let the monkey out of the cage!" he said. "Yes Chef," I replied, and he walked off with his big chef's hat and head in the air. Then I felt safe as he'd had his say on the matter and I knew he wouldn't be back.

Of course, my friendly kitchen pals thought it was very funny but it was quite tame compared to what we did to some of the other chefs. And it was not my last clash with Monsieur Le Fèvre.

# ESCARGOT BOURGUIGNONNE

## INGREDIENTS

¼ cup butter
2 shallots, very finely diced
2 cloves garlic, finely chopped
1 lb mushrooms, sliced
1 cup red wine
24 canned snails (drained)
2 cups Basic Brown Sauce (see recipe page 130)
1 sheet puff pastry
1 egg, beaten

## METHOD

**Melt** the butter in a sauté pan and then add the shallots, garlic, and mushrooms. Sauté until cooked. Add the red wine and reduce by half.

**Add** the escargot and Brown Sauce and cook for a further 5 minutes over medium heat. Divide the mixture equally into 4 dishes, 6 snails in each, with the sauce, and leave to cool.

**Cut** the sheet of puff pastry into 5-inch by 5-inch squares. Drape a piece of puff pastry over each dish and brush with beaten egg.

Cook for approximately 10 minutes at **350°F** or until the pastry is brown. Serve.

**Serves 4.**

*It's important not to overcook the escargot as they can become rather chewy.*

*The idea of the puff pastry is when the guest breaks through the puff pastry, you will get a beautiful aroma from the red wine. It's a nice touch to your dinner party.*

*At the restaurant we use Lion Head soup bowls, 10 fl oz, which work very well. They are quite common soup bowls and are available in most stores.*

*Alternatively, use a soup bowl of your choice, as long as it's not too big around the top so the puff pastry can fold over the top.*

*I prefer to drape the pastry on the bowl so that it's not too fancy and you have a more rustic look.*

# MOULES MARINIERE

## INGREDIENTS

3 lb fresh mussels
2 shallots, finely chopped
2 cloves garlic, finely chopped
1 tbsp olive oil
1 cup dry white wine
1 cup heavy cream
¼ cup parsley, chopped

## METHOD

**Wash** and clean the mussels and discard any mussels that are open.

**Using** a heavy bottom saucepan, add the shallots, garlic, olive oil, white wine and the mussels. Place a lid on the pot and put over a high heat. Cook for approximately 5 minutes or until the mussels are open. Keep checking during cooking. Remove from the heat using a slotted spoon to place the mussels into a bowl. Cover to keep them warm but leave the sauce in the saucepan.

**Place** the saucepan back onto the heat, add the cream and reduce the sauce by half. Pour the sauce over the mussels, sprinkle with the chopped parsley and serve.

**Serves 4.**

*It's very important that the mussels are fresh – if any are open before being cooked, they are dead, so throw them away. When cooking the mussels it's a good idea to shake the pan a couple of times with the lid on so that the mussels open up evenly. Keep the mussels covered at all times as they do tend to go cold very fast. I prefer to use a dry white wine as anything sweeter will change the taste.*

*Best served with plenty of hot crispy French bread – delicious!*

# OYSTERS MOSCOW

## INGREDIENTS

24 oysters of your choice
2 tomatoes, peeled and diced (see Method)
¾ cup vodka
6 tsp prepared horseradish
6 tsp sour cream
1 cup parsley, chopped
Crushed ice

## METHOD

**Open** the oysters. Loosen from their shells and refrigerate.

**Prepare** the tomatoes by plunging them into boiling water for about 1 minute. Take out of the pan and place into cold water. When cooled, cut into two, peel and remove the seeds. Dice the flesh into ¼-inch pieces.

**Assemble** the oysters by spooning 1 tsp of vodka over each oyster. Add ¼ tsp of horseradish and then place ¼ tsp of sour cream on each oyster. Sprinkle the diced tomatoes on top and then add a touch of parsley.

**Place** crushed ice on a large plate. Arrange the oysters on top and serve.

**Serves 4.**

*Use the oyster of your choice and when in season.*

*If you wish, you can put a cloth napkin on the plate below the crushed ice – this helps the ice from sliding around when serving.*

*A normal serving is 6 oysters per person.*

*I found the idea for this recipe about 20 years ago in Gourmet Magazine and it has been a favourite of mine ever since. It's a dish to spice up the oysters and make them drunk and fancy!*

# The Midland Hotel 2
## more Manchester Trainee Catastrophes

Working in a large kitchen with so many chefs was so different and less friendly than my previous experience at the Fishermans Arms where all the staff had become a close-knit group. So when I was a commis (apprentice) chef at the Midland Hotel my best friends were limited to the other trainee chefs.

All the trainees were in the same boat working split shifts which ran from 10 AM to 3 PM, and then 5:30 PM to 10 PM. We caught a bus to and from work so at the afternoon break we would walk around the city or sit in the YMCA café next door. Within a short time we became great pals and passed the time scheming up little tricks to amuse ourselves. Our favourite targets were the new trainees.

For example, we would send them to the bakery or pastry kitchen for a "long stand" or "white colouring". But if they were a little cheeky or big-headed they would be nabbed in the changing rooms, stripped naked and their private parts covered in shoe polish or bright red cochineal colouring from the kitchen. This kept them in place for some time!

The trainees all had to work in a section from the "hot kitchen" — one of Potatoes and Vegetables, Grill and Roast, Soup and Egg, Fish, or Sauce, as well as the larder. Training consisted of approximately six months on each section.

Of all the sections, the "veg corner" was the busiest as it covered the two restaurants and all the banquets so it had the most trainees working. As luck would have it, the section leader, or Chef de Partie, was the least pleasant of all the chefs. He would shout and punch your arm if you weren't fast enough and, although only around twenty-five years of age, had a well-developed nasty attitude towards the trainees.

Then one day out of the blue he announced he had been offered a better job and was leaving. This was music to our ears but as I had already suffered for nearly six months taking his abuse I felt it was high time for revenge.

Following a number of secret meetings we executed our plan. To start, six of us grabbed him in the changing room, stripped him down and applied a thorough coat of boot polish. We then stuffed him into a linen basket which was crammed into the service elevator and housekeeping rung to pick him up on the top floor. Needless to say we really felt he had his just desserts for the hell he gave us over the years — it was the perfect parting gift!

You should know that we rarely had to resort to such drastic measures. Most of the chefs were really quite decent and were happy to pass on their knowledge to me as I was eager to learn as much as I could.

We had one chef, Bob Livingstone, who was not only a decent man but also extremely talented. But for some strange reason Monsieur Le Fèvre, the head chef, wasn't too fond of him. I don't really know why but regardless he was my hero in the kitchen and I learnt a great deal from him.

One day we were working on a large banquet and Bob asked me to put the potatoes on the top shelf of the heating trolley and the veg on the lower part. In the middle of the job Monsieur Le Fèvre came along and told me to switch the two. I had more sense than to argue but as I was changing it Bob came along and asked me what was I doing. After explaining myself he said, "I don't care. This is my job so change it back." When Monsieur Le Fèvre returned a short time later he said, "Mr Fooler, you are hard of hearing now?" and I replied, "No, chef, I'm only doing what I was told by Bob." He asked me who I worked for and by this time I was really shaking and said, "You, chef," and proceeded to change it again.

The banquet went off without any more hitches and the rest of the evening I worked on the line in the main kitchen. Then I noticed Bob waiting outside the chef de cuisine's office.

Monsieur Le Fèvre came along strutting like an old peacock with his high hat on and asked Bob into his office. I thought, "Oh no!! What's going to happen now?" Within five minutes I heard Monsieur Le Fèvre shout and then all his gold medals come flying out the open door. "These mean nothing to me," he said, "but what does mean a lot is that I am the executive chef of this hotel and what I say goes." So that was that. He got his message over very clear and I kept out of his way for at least two weeks.

Another catastrophe I had with Monsieur Le Fèvre was when I worked on the Grill and Roast section. The section had a very large roasting oven with six shelves inside, each of which could hold a large roasting pan with eight whole chickens. The shelves rotated so when you wanted to get anything out ou had to stop the shelves from rotating before removing a single tray of chickens.

On one occasion, as I was pulling the roasting tray out I misplaced my hand on one of the handles and it started burning me. We were always taught that the best thing to do was to put it down fast but tip the tray away so the grease wouldn't splash and burn even more.

In spite of my training that's exactly what happened as I dropped the tray and splashed fat all over the floor. Then as I picked the tray up out of the corner of my eye I saw Monsieur Le Fèvre strutting quickly towards me. Before I could shout a warning he went down with his legs in the air and his back in the hot grease. All I could hear was, "Fooler! Fooler!" so I immediately hid behind the big oven out of sight. To say the least, he was not amused. The sous chef found me cowering behind the oven and told me to take a break in the cafeteria. I did not have to be told twice and scuppered away. I kept out of his way for many days but every time he saw me in the distance all I heard was, "Fooler, you fool me!"

# SAUTÉED CALAMARI & SHRIMP

## INGREDIENTS

¼ cup olive oil
2 cloves garlic, finely chopped
¼ cup unsalted butter
12 shrimp (16-20 count), deveined and peeled
*1 lb calamari, cut into rings, approximately ¼-inch thick
¼ cup white wine
Juice of 1 lemon
1 tbsp chopped parsley

## METHOD

**In** a large sauté pan, place the olive oil, garlic and butter and heat until the butter bubbles in the pan.
**Put** the shrimp in the pan and sauté for approximately 3 minutes and then add the calamari and sauté for another 2 minutes.
**Add** the white wine and cook for a further 2 minutes until the shrimp and calamari are cooked.
**Squeeze** the lemon juice over the dish and add the chopped parsley.
**Divide** into 4 equal portions and serve with bread for mopping up the sauce.
**Serves 4.**

*Ask the fishmonger to clean the calamari for you if it's fresh as it is quite a messy job.*

*The 16-20 count shrimp are a good size to use as the cooking time with the calamari is perfect. If the shrimp are too small, they will overcook.*

*\* It is quite acceptable to use frozen calamari for this dish.*

# BEEF WELLINGTON

## INGREDIENTS

2 lbs centre cut tenderloin of beef
¼ cup butter
1 small onion, chopped
1 clove garlic, minced
½ lb button mushrooms
½ cup sweet sherry (Harveys Bristol Cream)
¼ cup fresh white bread crumbs
1 sheet puff pastry
1 egg, beaten
1 cup Red Wine Sauce (see recipe page 144)

## METHOD

**Put** a drop of oil in a sauté pan and when hot place in the tenderloin and seal it on all sides; remove from pan and leave to rest.

**Add** the butter to the pan and add the onions, garlic and mushrooms. Sauté until the onions and mushrooms begin to brown. Add the sweet sherry and reduce until the mushrooms are drunk and dry. Place the mushroom mixture into a food processor with the bread crumbs and pulse the processor about 3 times so it breaks up but is not too mushy. Place into a refrigerator to cool.

**Place** the puff pastry sheet on a lightly floured table and egg wash the edges of the puff pastry. Place the mushroom mixture down the centre of the puff pastry about 2-inches wide and the length of your tenderloin leaving a 1½-inch space at each end. Place the tenderloin on the top of the mushroom mix and fold the puff pastry around the beef (first the sides, then the ends) to form a log. Place onto a baking sheet with folded edges down. Egg wash the wellington and place into a preheated oven at **380°F** until the pastry is brown, about 10-15 minutes. Keep an eye on the wellington to make sure the pastry does not burn. The beef will be medium rare.

**Remove** from the oven and leave to rest for 5 minutes. Carve into 4 equal pieces and serve atop Red Wine Sauce. **Serves 4.**

*It is important that you use a good quality of beef for this recipe. It will make all the difference to the overall taste of this famous dish. I make this dish every New Year's Eve at the restaurant.*

*It is a lot easier to let the beef and the mushroom mix go cold as it's important that the puff pastry does not come into contact with any heat while making the wellington.*

*To make egg wash just whisk one egg in a bowl. A lot of chefs put milk into the egg but I prefer a deeper colour with just the egg.*

# CALYPSO CHICKEN WITH WILD MUSHROOMS

## INGREDIENTS

1 lb unsalted butter, divided
4 oz shitake mushrooms, finely sliced
4 oz oyster mushrooms, finely sliced
4 oz button mushrooms, finely sliced
1 cup onion, diced
2 cloves garlic, minced
½ cup sherry (Harveys Bristol Cream)
4 (8 oz) chicken breasts
1 lb breadcrumbs or Panko
2 cups Lemon Butter Sauce (see recipe page 136)

## METHOD

**Melt** ½ cup butter in a pan over moderate heat. Add the mushrooms, onion, and garlic and sauté until they are slightly cooked. Add the sherry and reduce until all the sherry has evaporated. Leave to one side until you are ready to fill the chicken breasts.

**Place** the chicken breast on a cutting board and with a small paring knife make a small incision in the top end of the plump side of the breast. Slowly ease your knife down the middle of the breast to make a long pocket, being careful not to tear the chicken. With a spoon, fill the breast with mushrooms by edging the spoon into the pocket slowly and try to keep the breast whole.

**Melt** the rest of the butter in a pan and pour into a dish. Place the breadcrumbs in a dish next to the melted butter. Carefully take the chicken breast and coat with the butter and then the breadcrumbs. Repeat this process twice and then lay the breast on a buttered tray. Pour any remaining butter over the breasts.

**Place** into the oven at **350°F** for approximately 20 minutes, until cooked through. The chicken should turn a golden brown colour.

**Before** serving, cut the chicken on an angle into 2 pieces and arrange on the plate with the Lemon Butter Sauce.

**Serves 4.**

*When buying the chicken breasts, make sure they are plump. It will make it easier to make a pocket for the mushrooms.*

*This recipe requires lots of extra breadcrumbs in the bowl to prevent clumps.*

*This is a good method of cooking chicken breasts as it keeps the chicken breast moist and tender. Also, you can cook the chicken without the filling and then serve it with fresh asparagus to make Chicken Princess.*

*I prefer this method when cooking banquets as chicken breasts tend to dry. This method keeps the chicken moist.*

# Hollins College
## The Toast Rack, Manchester

Anyone who has lived in Manchester will be familiar with Hollins College, more commonly known as The Toast Rack due to its iconic shape. As mentioned previously, when I was at the Midland Hotel in Manchester I went to Hollins part-time where I worked one day per week with the famous chef, Jack Neighbour. I'll always be grateful for his guidance and help during that early period of my career.

Part of my City & Guilds exam at the college was an assessment throughout the year but the advanced final exam was a one-day six-hour marathon including both written and practical tests. That's where Jack Neighbour came into the picture as you had to have certain skills to get through the exam. I do believe we had twelve students start the class but ended with only six people taking the exam as Jack had little patience for stragglers.

The day of the six-hour final arrived and we were escorted into the exam room with our Escoffier cookbooks in hand. There was a large blackboard at the front of the class and when I glanced at it my heart sank. It was a long menu with some extremely tricky recipes — each with a set time to prepare and serve just for added pressure.

For example, one of the dishes was Fresh Shrimp Bisque; in those days blenders were rare and I had never even used one before! But I spotted a blender at the top of the kitchen and had the good sense to figure out that it was for blending the soup. Then there was Braised Lettuce stuffed with Rice a la Grecque. That was the hardest dish to get right so it didn't look like something the dog dragged in. Even the potatoes were not simple. They asked for Pomme Dauphinoise which is potato puree mixed with choux pastry (the dough used to make chocolate eclairs or cream puffs).

Let's just say if you didn't have the skills to make these dishes you were in deep trouble.

Desserts weren't required on this exam as there was another final for pastry only. But we did make Spinach Soufflé with Anchovies which was tricky enough. With the anchovies right in the middle your mix had to be perfect in order for it to rise properly. I'll never forget that dish because my serving bowl was dirty and as I tried to wipe it clean my soufflé started to fall. The examiner took a spoon, went right into the middle and took out a big chunk. He didn't even taste it; he just wanted to see whether I had cooked it correctly and I breathed a huge sigh of relief when I passed even with a half-deflated soufflé.

All in all it was an experience I would never want to go through again. Throughout the entire day the examiner walked around writing notes, which was quite nerve-wracking as you had no idea how you were doing. The only good thing was they weren't interested in your cleaning skills. Each student was appointed a lady to do the washing up and to keep their station tidy. Just to be safe, though, I made it quite clear to my helper she was not to pick up or wash any pan I had not given her!

The final straw came when I was ready for the last stage of the Pomme Dauphinoise which is frying. I was just checking my pan to see if the oil was hot enough. Keep in mind we could not use fryers as they were testing our skill in cooking with a friture (a pan of oil on the stove). When I looked across the kitchen I saw another student whose fat wasn't hot enough and it was coming right over the top of the fryer. The examiner asked him if he had any more mix left and he said no. The examiner apologized but asked him to leave the kitchen immediately so he was failed on the spot. I can't tell you the feeling of panic I felt when the examiner looked at mine!

As it was, to my immense relief, my dish turned out perfectly. Not only was I was extremely happy but I believe Chef Jack Neighbour was happy, too, as it had been a year of hard work for both of us leading up to that final moment of success.

# CHILEAN SEABASS
# WITH SWEET CORN SALSA & CHIPOTLE SAUCE

## INGREDIENTS

1½ cups sweet corn kernels, fresh or frozen
1 red pepper, ¼-inch diced
1 small onion, ¼-inch diced
2 tbsp fresh cilantro, chopped
1 tbsp honey
2 tbsp olive oil
1 tbsp rice wine vinegar
Salt and pepper
4 (6 oz) Chilean seabass fillets
2 cups Chipotle Sauce (see recipe page 134)

## METHOD

**Toss** the corn kernels with a touch of oil, spread onto a baking tray and roast in a **350°F** oven for 10 minutes.

**In** a bowl, add the warm sweet corn, red pepper, onion and fresh cilantro. Add the honey, olive oil and rice vinegar and mix well. Add salt and pepper to your taste and leave in the fridge until needed.

**Season** the seabass with salt and pepper. Heat a sauté pan with olive oil and let it get quite hot. Add the seabass and brown on both sides. Place in the oven at **350°F** to finish the cooking – approximately 6-8 minutes. Check the fish for doneness by pressing the top slightly – it should be quite firm to the touch.

**Place** the fish onto 4 plates and spoon the salsa equally onto each fish. Ladle the Chipotle Sauce around the fish and serve.

**Serves 4.**

*The seabass fillets come in various thickness and so you will have to adjust the cooking time accordingly.*

*The salsa is served chilled with the fish. The taste goes wonderfully with the fish.*

*The Chipotle Sauce compliments this dish very well.*

*Halibut can be used instead of seabass as a good substitute.*

# CRISPY MANGO SHRIMP

This dish has been on the menu since Day 1 and is very popular with the guests who visit Calypso Grill frequently.

## INGREDIENTS

1 cup mango chutney
½ cup butter
½ cup vegetable stock
¼ cup rum (optional)
2 lb large shrimp (8-12 shrimp/lb)
2 tsp Scotch Bonnet sauce
1 lemon, juice
1 cup white wine
1 cup corn starch
1 cup all purpose flour
Soy bean or corn oil for frying

## METHOD

**Place** the mango chutney, butter, vegetable stock and rum into a sauce pan and bring to the boil. STIR ALL THE TIME to prevent sticking to the pan. Lower the heat and simmer for about 10 minutes on low heat. The mango sauce should not be a thick consistency – it should just coat the shrimp.

**Peel** and devein the shrimp leaving the tails intact. In a bowl, combine the Scotch Bonnet sauce, lemon juice and white wine and then add the shrimp. Leave in the marinade until ready to cook – approximately 15 minutes.

**Blend** together the corn starch and flour and coat each shrimp in the mixture, shaking off any excess.

**Prepare** a deep fryer or put around 3-inches of soybean oil, or corn oil, in a Dutch oven. Heat the oil over a moderate heat and check the temperature by putting a piece of bread in the oil – it should start slowly browning (around **350°F**).

**Place** each shrimp, one by one, into the pan or fryer, with a maximum of 6 at a time. Turn the shrimp with a slotted spoon so they brown evenly and cook for roughly 7 minutes total. If they brown too fast, it means the oil is too hot. It is important to heat the oil to the correct temperature. When nicely browned and crispy, take the shrimp out of the oil and place on paper towel to drain.

**Arrange** the shrimp onto 4 plates and spoon the mango sauce over top to serve.

**Serves 4.**

*This recipe works well with large shrimp. I recommend 8-12 shrimp to the pound, but if they are larger they will also work well. Smaller shrimp can still be used but you will lose the flavour of the dish as you need to taste the shrimp with the mango sauce – if the shrimp are too small you will just taste the mango sauce.*

# DUCK BREASTS IN GRAND MARNIER WITH CRANBERRIES

## INGREDIENTS

4 (8 oz) duck breasts
2 oranges, peeled and segmented
¼ cup Grand Marnier
1 cup Basic Brown Sauce (see recipe page 130)
¼ cup fresh or frozen whole cranberries

## METHOD

**Place** the duck breasts into a cold sauté pan, skin side down. Cook the breasts on high heat for 8-10 minutes or until the skin is brown and crispy. Turn over for 2 more minutes then remove from the pan. You can test the duck by feeling the breast – if it's very rare it will spring back from the touch. If you need the duck more cooked, place it back into the pan until it feels more firm. Keep the cooked breasts in a warm place to rest for at least 5 minutes or until you finish the sauce.

**To make the sauce,** remove the fat from the pan but leave the tasty bits on the bottom. Place the pan back on the heat. Add the Grand Marnier and Basic Brown Sauce. Stir and scrape up the tasty bits. Reduce this mixture until it coats the back of a spoon. Add the cranberries and cook a further 2 minutes.

**To serve,** slice the duck on an angle into 4 slices. Place on the plate and lightly coat with the sauce. Place the orange segments atop the duck and serve immediately with the potatoes of your choice and fresh vegetables.
**Serves 4.**

*It is important to place the duck breasts in the cold pan when you cook them. No oil is needed as there is plenty of fat in the skin.*

*I prefer duck to be cooked pink as in my opinion the longer they are cooked the tougher they are. Also, the resting of the duck is very important (resting will tenderise the meat).*

*I season my duck breast with salt and pepper before I cook them but this is your preference.*

# The Days of Jack Blunk

Towards the end of my career in the U.K. I worked in a small restaurant called Blunks which is situated in Waltham Abbey in Essex. Sad to say, when I was visiting there recently I discovered it is now an everyday Chinese restaurant, however when I worked there it was a very prestigious fish restaurant.

The entrance featured a tile and wood floor that absolutely gleamed. I remember Vera the cleaner polishing on her hands and knees — no fancy machine for her. The restaurant had twelve tables for two plus four larger tables for parties of four or more. The tables were solid oak and also highly polished. Then there was a door leading into the kitchen with its own stable door and shelf near the bottom for serving the food.

Next to the kitchen entrance there was an archway with steps leading to the bar and seating area. There was also a large stable door with a top that opened into the street which was great during the summer months. The seating area included three large tables with pews on either side which looked rather rustic and had red-chequered table cloths; with the polished stone floor it provided a beautiful contrasting view.

The bar of course was highly polished wood and mirrors with crystal glassware so you can imagine how fancy that appeared. Next to the bar were three steps leading into the kitchen which again had a stable door with the top always open during service. The beauty of this was we had a view of the customers while they could also see us.

Jack Blunk was the owner and a very flamboyant man. He often called me to the door to tell customers as they entered, "This is my chef. He cooks like a dream and you'll have a wonderful experience tonight." Jack was quite a character and I found him extremely amusing during the three years I worked for him.

I must point out that this restaurant was not cheap — in fact Jack was way ahead of his time as the Ritz in London would have been on par. We had a lot of high rollers as customers.

We served mostly fish like Dover sole, whole turbot, and whole halibut but Maine lobster was also a specialty. We had an oak cabinet refrigerator with a glass lid so we would display the fish every evening and I must say it looked very impressive. When Jack was taking an order he would bring the whole fish out of the cabinet and place it on the table. He even pulled out a scale to give an idea of the cost — not cheap. He would also throw live lobsters on the table much to the horror of the ladies. And although it gave me a laugh when a lobster started walking on the table towards a guest, sometimes the customer was not so amused.

We had meat on the menu too — sirloin steak was the best seller. To tenderise the beef we hung our steak on the bone in the fridge which is what the butcher would do in years gone by. These days it's all done by lamps and temperature stages in the coolers.

When Jack was in the mood he would have his chefs bring down the whole rib of beef. This would be one hell of a size and he would explain how long the meat had been hanging and the side the last steak was taken from. The meat would get black and of course we would trim off the end before cutting out the steak. But a lot of our guests would look at it and say, "Sounds very nice but I prefer a Dover sole tonight!"

Blunks is where I met my good friend, Eddie, who worked with me in the kitchen. We really enjoyed working with Jack and I can assure you we had some good laughs. There was one evening when Jack decided to bring in an accordion player who sat on a stool playing Parisian French music. The restaurant was very busy so of course so were we. As I said previously, we had a lot of high rollers in the restaurant and the waiter said there was a "nice Rolls" outside, which meant a Rolls Royce. We did not get many of those parked outside the restaurant so we were looking around to see if we could guess who it belonged to.

As the night went on and everybody went home the Rolls Royce was still outside and we were baffled. It turned out to be the accordion player's car! So we said "Hell mate, what are you doing this for?" And he said, he enjoyed it and did it for pleasure. He just loved playing the accordion! Needless to say every time he played Jack had a great story telling everyone where the French music was coming from — the man with the Rolls Royce.

Once, on my day off, Jack called to ask if I would come in for a few hours to help Eddie in the kitchen. I must point out it was not an easy kitchen to work on your own as the food was made with a lot of detail and it was important to have every dish precise.

So I came in as I knew the customer very well and I knew he would be expecting to see me and was bringing ten people for dinner. This guy was a trip — he also had a Rolls Royce and a very highly strung Irish wife who I thought was very charming although she often had trouble with her husband, Bill.

They all arrived at the restaurant and Bill came into the kitchen and gave us each a £20 tip before he even ordered any food. He said it was always best to keep the chefs sweet. So Jack was taking the orders for the starter and they were artistic in their own rights. We had amazing Smoked Salmon, King Prawns (around six ounces each) and a great Duck Terrine which Eddie made regularly. I was preparing all these dishes when I suddenly heard Jack shout, "Chef! Chef! Stop the orders now!" I went running to the door to see what was wrong. He said, "Stop — these guests have come to the wrong restaurant! They are looking for a steak house. Would you like me to book a steak house?" And he pulled out his phone.

Bill's wife stood up and I could see she was mad as hell and shouted that she did not need to be insulted by this "ugly little man" and then she said they'd go somewhere else to eat.

Bill said, "You can go but I'm staying right here where we are." She replied, "We're going where we can get better food." Then all the women left and the men stayed with us for dinner.

What happened was they had ordered six steaks out of 10 orders and Jack told them he was a famous fish restaurant and if they all wanted steak then they were in the wrong restaurant. We all laughed in the kitchen as we all knew how ballsey he was but that one was his best yet.

Afterwards, Bill and his male guests announced they had a great meal and it tasted even better without the women. Just as he said that his wife walked back into the restaurant obviously very upset with Jack and threw some money at him. She said, "It's not because of the money we did not eat here tonight it was because of the insults you gave to my friends and me." Jack picked up the money and all he said was, "Thank you very much." Needless to say we did not see Bill, or his wife, much after that.

There was rarely a dull moment at the restaurant as Jack used to keep us all amused one way or another. But Jack wasn't the only one we had to deal with — we

also had a kitchen porter named Alan. One day I had to make a cake for my cousin's 21st birthday. We wanted it made with the colours of the West Ham United football team and knew it wasn't going to be easy. I wasn't very good at cakes, especially decorating them, but Eddie was good so we decided to transform a fruit cake bought from Jackson's, the bakery, or Harrods. Eddie did his magic and we changed its colours to claret and blue — the West Ham colours. I was taking it up to my cousin's the next day so I asked Alan the kitchen porter to put it in my car for me.

That evening when I got home I went into the back of the car for the cake — nothing there. I checked in the trunk and throughout the car — nothing. So I rang Eddie thinking Alan had misheard and put it in his car instead of mine. Nothing there either. So where the hell was it? The next morning we grabbed Alan to ask where he put the cake and he swore on a stack of Bibles he'd put it on the back seat of my car. So there we were — no cake and a 21st birthday that very day!

Eddie suggested we ring the police station and ask if anybody had found a birthday cake. I said they'd think us crazy but we called all the same and were told that a gentleman had just brought a West Ham coloured cake into the station.

It turned out this fellow had found it on the back seat of his car and knew somebody would be missing it. So the day was saved and needless to say Alan was not to be trusted again. His excuse was it was dark outside! Really!

# FISHCAKES

## INGREDIENTS

1 lb fish
¼ cup butter
1 clove garlic, minced
1 tbsp mixed herbs
1 cup white wine
½ cup mayonnaise
1 tbsp Dijon mustard
2 tsp Worcestershire sauce
4 cups breadcrumbs or Panko, divided
2 cups flour
2 eggs, beaten
2 cups Caper Sauce (see recipe page 134) or
2 cups Herb Butter Sauce (see recipe page 136)

## METHOD

**Place** the fish and the butter into an oven-proof dish. Add the garlic, chopped herbs and white wine. Cover the dish with tin foil and place into the oven for approximately 15 minutes at **350°F** or until the fish is cooked.

**Take** the fish out of the dish and place in a mixing bowl.

**Place** the liquid from the dish into a sauté pan and reduce into a glaze. Add to the fish once it is cooled.

**Add** the mayonnaise, mustard, Worcestershire sauce and ½ cup of the breadcrumbs and mix together. Be careful not to mash the fish too finely. Form into 8 cakes and refrigerate for 15 minutes to chill.

**Prepare** 3 bowls – one for the flour, one for the beaten eggs and one for the breadcrumbs. Place each fishcake into the flour, then the egg and then the breadcrumbs. Reshape them into cakes and refrigerate again for 30 minutes.

**There** are two ways to cook the fishcakes: deep fry or shallow fry in a sauté pan. Shallow frying keeps the fishcakes less greasy, however we do deep fry them at the restaurant and they turn out very well.

**Serve** the fishcakes, 2 per plate, with either Caper Sauce or Herb Butter Sauce.

**Serves 4.**

*It's important not to mash the fish when making the fishcakes. It's better to have flakes of the fish in the cake.*

*The type of fish to use would be fresh tuna, wahoo, mahimahi or cold water fish: cod, haddock or salmon. It is entirely up to you.*

*For the breadcrumbs, I prefer to use Panko.*

# GRILLED GINGER TUNA
# WITH GINGER SAUCE

## INGREDIENTS

1 tbsp fresh stem ginger, peeled and chopped fine
1 cup soy sauce
¼ cup sugar
½ cup pineapple juice
¼ cup rice vinegar
1 tsp dried chilli peppers
2 tbsp sherry (Harveys Bristol Cream)
½ cup vegetable stock
2 tbsp cornstarch
4 (8 oz) tuna steaks
2 tbsp oil

## METHOD

**In** a large saucepan, mix together fresh ginger, soy sauce, sugar, pineapple juice, rice vinegar, dried chile peppers, sherry and vegetable stock.

**Remove** ½ of this mixture and place in a bowl to one side. This is the marinade for the tuna.

**Boil** the other ½ of the mixture for about 2 minutes and then mix the cornstarch really well with a little water and add very slowly to the pot. You do not want the sauce to be too thick. Cover and leave to the side of the stove.

**Marinate** the tuna filets for 15 minutes in the marinade you saved, then remove the tuna and discard the marinade.

**Heat** a grill or grill pan then pour 2 tbsp oil in the bottom. Add the tuna steaks and cook to your liking, but I recommend no more than medium-rare, which will be 2 minutes on each side in a hot pan.

**Place** a small amount of the Ginger Sauce on each plate and the tuna on top. Serve.

**Serves 4.**

*As always, use the freshest fish for this dish. Ideally, your steak should be around ½-inch thick.*
*Do not leave the fish in the marinade for longer than 15 minutes as the mixture could dry out the fish.*
*Make sure the grill pan is hot when you are ready to use it, as this helps seal the fish.*

# LEMON SOLE STUFFED WITH CRAB & SPINACH

## INGREDIENTS

1 lb Crabcakes mixture (see recipe page 36)
8 sole fillets
Kosher salt
12 oz fresh spinach
¾ cup cold unsalted butter, cut into cubes
2 shallots, finely chopped
½ cup dry white wine
½ cup vegetable or fish stock
1 cup heavy cream

## METHOD

**Make** the Crabcakes recipe and divide into 8 cakes and refrigerate until needed.

**Lay** the sole fillets on the board and season with salt.

**Cook** the spinach by plunging into boiling water for 10 seconds and then strain in a colander. Refresh the spinach in cold water to stop it from cooking and to keep the colour.

Squeeze the excess water out of the spinach and divide it into 8 balls.

**Place** the spinach on the fish evenly and place the crabcakes on the spinach. Roll the fillet tight and secure with a toothpick.

**Lightly** butter an ovenproof dish and place the fish fillets in the dish. Add the chopped shallots, white wine and stock. Cover with foil and cook in the oven for approximately 15 minutes at **350°F.** When cooked, place the fish onto a plate, cover with the foil, and keep in a warm place.

**Pour** the liquid from the dish that the fish was cooked in into a sauce pan and bring to a boil. Add the heavy cream and reduce until the liquid is halved. This will thicken slightly. Take the pan off the heat and add the butter, one cube at a time, and then whisk until all the butter has mixed into the sauce.

**Place** 2 fish servings per plate. Pour the sauce over the fish and serve.

**Serves 4.**

*Use lemon sole fillets or Dover sole fillets. Sole is inclined to shrink when cooking using this method. Cover the fillet with cling film and bang it slightly with the flat of a knife, just to break the tissue a little.*

*When adding butter to your sauce, make sure the pan is off the heat otherwise the sauce will split.*

*When making the sauce, always use a thick bottomed pan and always keep stirring to prevent burning. There are pots available on the market with copper bottoms – they are a great investment for making sauces.*

*When cooking, I prefer to use unsalted butter so it is up to the individual how much salt you would like to use in the dish.*

# CHEFS CHOICE

| | |
|---|---|
| CALYPSO FISHCAKES | 12⁵⁰ |
| TUNA SASHIMI | 12⁰⁰ |
| CHICKEN LIVER PATE | 10⁰⁰ |
| SAUTEED CALAMARI & SHRIMP | 14⁰⁰ |
| GRILLED KING SHRIMP W/LIME-HERB BUTTER | 16⁰⁰ |
| ARUGULA, BEET, SQUASH & GOAT CHEESE | 11⁰⁰ |

## CHEFS CHOICE

WILD MUSHROOM TART W/ARUGULA   14⁵⁰

CALYPSO FISHCAKES   12⁵⁰

TUNA SASHIMI

CHICKEN LIVER PATE

# Prospect Reef

## Tortola, BVI

After my stint at Blunks in Waltham Abbey in Essex, and at the ripe age of 26, I felt I was approaching the height of my career and started to look for a job as chef in a larger establishment.

Coincidentally, my good friend Eddie who also worked at Blunks, was offered the chef's position at a country club just outside of London. As luck would have it, the owner of the club also owned Prospect Reef Resort on the British Virgin Island of Tortola and they were looking for a new head chef. To my delight and surprise I was offered the position and was soon on my way to a new adventure.

Tortola itself was beautiful — I used to say it reminded me of the Bounty chocolate bar ads on TV in the UK. The bars are filled with coconut and they were portrayed with a model sitting beneath a palm tree on a Caribbean island.

This was the start of my long journey throughout the Caribbean and little did I know that I was in for one hell of a culture shock.

The first thing I noticed was the heat. I had been to sun destinations before while on vacation but working in the heat was another thing entirely. A kitchen is a pretty hot place anyway so you can imagine adding the heat from a blazing sun throughout the day with nothing but some overhead fans for cooling. With the exception of the heat, the kitchen was more or less the same as most. Of course, looking out over the crystal waters of the Caribbean Sea was also a nice change!

Then there was the different culture of the Caribbean people. Unlike the kitchens in the UK, where during my training years I found little respect amongst co-workers, here I discovered there were no raised voices and not much call for it either. This allowed me to use a fresh new approach in my job which reflected the way of life there — you respected your co-workers and they gave respect back.

Across from the resort there was a hotel called Fort Burt where the owner's son opened a disco. We danced until we dropped — those were the days! There was also an open-air disco right next door to the local bakery and at two or three in the morning we bought fresh bread to take home. What a delicious way to end the night!

I lived in a small suite on the harbour where a lady named Miss Robbie had a fishing boat. This boat had all the bells and whistles including an air-conditioned cabin. One day there was a mahimahi fishing tournament and Miss Robbie was kind enough to invite me.

But the problem was that I was "on the razzle" the night before and with virtually no sleep felt truly awful. I immediately went into the air-conditioned cabin after I was allocated a rod thinking that if by some miracle my hook caught a fish they would call me to the chair to reel it in. Then Murphy's Law struck as every time I laid my head down a fish would bite and I had to stagger out to the deck to heave it in. At the end of the day I won the tournament!

One of the most spectacular moments of the day was seeing a school of dolphins swimming by the boat doing all their tricks for us. It was absolutely brilliant, but the captain said we had to get away from them because dolphins send a signal to the fish not to bite the bait. I'm still not sure if he was pulling my leg as I've never heard that since!

Finally, I must mention the day American President Jimmy Carter, his wife Rosalind and their son visited the island. Miss Robbie was good friends with the president and had arranged to take them out fishing. Imagine my delight when she asked me to prepare a lunch of "finger foods" for their excursion. So I made a variety of small tarts, open-faced sandwiches and the president's favourite — strawberry tarts (he ate four of them!) At the end of the day President Carter asked Miss Robbie to take him to Prospect Reef to have a drink with the chef who made his lunch. It was a day I'll never forget, ending with Rosalind Carter asking me many questions about my career. Little did I realize it was just the beginning of my journey through the Caribbean.

**V·I· ISLAND FOODS**

# CHEF GEORGE

By Mary Grimes

Candles flicker in the evening breeze, harbor lights glitter below, tables set with gleaming crystal provide an evening of dining at the newly opened Harbour Restaurant at Prospect Reef.

Chef George, a genial Englishman, oversees the house specialty, lobster with three sauces, garnished with parsley, tomato rose, and scallops. The dish is delicate and arranged with artistry. The extensive menu receives his equal attention, all courses served with visual palatability as well as excellent good taste.

George Fowler, a student of culinary skills and kitchen management studied for seven years with British Transport Hotels, Manchester England to attain such high standards and practical expertise. "It was not easy," he says and the final examination after cooking under French chefs with advanced courses took three hours of written tests and a six hour preparation of foods to pass the critical eye of the examiners. With such credentials, George went to work in London for the exclusive Blunk's Restaurant, a French seafood house serving nothing but fresh foods prepared especially for intimate guests.

After several years in London it became a question whether to continue on or go abroad for more experience. Elihu Rhymer offered an opportunity to come to the Virgin Islands and head up the staff at Prospect Reef, while George was considering Australia. Tortola won out and the Pavillion Restaurant became George's next experience.

Adapting from the London bustle to the more gentle ways of Tortola was not an immediate transistion. "It took me at least a year to adjust to the climate and style of this tropical paradise." Working with the menu and staff, George has trained Clarence McCoy as second Chef for the Harbour Restaurant and Patrick Christopher to head the Pavillion Restaurant.

Harbour Restaurant will be open seven days a week, for dinner only, with Reuben playing accoustical guitar every Saturday evening.

*Chef George proudly presents his Lobster Champagne.*

George has trained his staff well, the food is of an excellent and high standard. The menu is extensive and enticing. Each dinner is started with complimentary fresh, raw vegetables and dip, and following the appetizers a small glass of sherbert is presented to freshen the palate. Each dish is prepared specially and adorned with George's signature, a tomato cut carefully to form a rose, with small basil leaves for accent.

The Pavillion Restaurant, a more informal atmosphere, is open also seven days a week serving breakfast, lunch, and dinner. Lunches feature crepes, fresh fish, curry chicken and fresh ground beef grilled at the barbeque. Thursday nights feature Barbeque and steel band and prime rib is the speciality on Sundays.

Where will George be off to after Tortola? "Singapore or work the Waldorf Astoria in New York." Meanwhile we have him bustling around Prospect Reef and off hours he can be found dancing at the disco, sailing at mid-night, or sharing 3 a.m. coffee and music with friends.

## LOBSTER CHAMPAGNE

1 2½ lb. local lobster
2 oz. chopped shallots
1 oz. butter
½ bottle champagne
½ pint double cream
¼ pint fish stock

### Fish Stock

Saute 1 lb. fish bones in butter with one lemon, 4 fluid oz. white wine, 1 medium onion and 2 bayleaves. Do not brown. Add 1 pint water and simmer for 20 minutes. Strain all ingredients into a clean pan and simmer the liquid until you are left with ¼ pint in the pan.

### Lobster

Boil the lobster and leave to cool when cooked. Saute the chopped shallots in butter without coloring and pour in the champagne. Simmer by half and add the double cream and fish stock. It is best to use a thick bottomed pan and simmer the sauce until it is a coating consistency. Season to taste.

Take the meat out of the lobster shell and cut into scallops. Gently heat the lobster meat in the sauce. Replace the meat into the shell and serve — with champagne, of course. **V.I.**

# LOBSTER & SHRIMP CHAMPAGNE

## INGREDIENTS

4 (8 oz) lobster tails
1 lb (16-20) black tiger shrimp, peeled and deveined
¼ cup butter
½ cup champagne
2 cups Butter Sauce (see recipe page 131)

## METHOD

**Take** the lobster meat out of the shell by cutting with a pair of scissors on the soft part of the shell, under the tail. Cut into 1-inch bite-size pieces and add the shrimp.

**Put** the butter into a sauté pan and when hot, add the lobster and shrimp and sauté over a medium to high heat for 3 minutes. Add the champagne to the lobster and shrimp. Continue cooking with the champagne and then add the butter sauce. Remove the lobster and shrimp from the pan. Cover and keep warm. Reduce the sauce until it coats the back of a spoon. Add the lobster and shrimp back into the sauce and serve.

**Serves 4.**

*Using a saucepan with a very thin bottom tends to burn the sauce when reducing it.*
*The quality of lobster can vary. At the restaurant we use Grade 1 Spiny Lobster Tail. This dish can also be used with Maine lobster.*
*It's OK to use inexpensive champagne.*

# PAELLA

To be honest, this dish really needs to be cooked in a round, shallow paella pan. This recipe is designed to serve 8-10 as paella is best when cooked in large amounts.

## INGREDIENTS

1 cup olive oil
2 cloves garlic, chopped fine
1 medium onion, ½-inch dice
1 small green pepper, ½-inch dice
1 small red pepper, ½-inch dice

½ lb boneless, skinless chicken thighs, 1-inch cubed
½ lb Italian sausage, skinned and broken up
1 lb chorizo sausage, skinned and ¼-inch sliced

1 cup green olives
1 (14 oz) can chickpeas, rinsed and strained
1 (14 oz) can artichoke hearts, cut into thirds

½ lb (16-20) shrimp, peeled and deveined
4 oz calamari, sliced
2 cups long grain white rice
4 cups chicken stock
Big pinch of saffron strands or powder

4 large tomatoes, ¾-inch dice
12 fresh mussels and/or clams (optional)

*It's important to make the paella in the stages I've set out for the dish to turn out correctly.*

*Have all the ingredients prepared before you begin cooking as once you start it goes fast.*

*Don't overheat the olive oil when starting the dish so that the oil doesn't burn. It's important to have the flavour of the olive oil as this is a Spanish dish.*

*I mix in a little yellow colouring (just a couple of drops) into the chicken stock to give the paella a little more 'posh' look.*

*With the dish having a fair amount of olive oil, some people prefer to eat paella with a squeeze of lemon.*

## METHOD

**Place** the paella pan over a moderate heat and heat the olive oil until hot but not smoking. Add the garlic, onion and peppers and sauté for 1 minute.

**Add** the chicken thighs, Italian sausage and the chorizo sausage. Saute until coated nicely with the oil and the ingredients are half-cooked.

**Add** the green olives, chickpeas and the artichoke hearts. Gently stir and sauté again until well coated with the oil.

**Stir** in the shrimp and calamari.

**Add** the rice and make sure it is well mixed in with the ingredients so that it collects all the flavours.

**Mix** the chicken stock and saffron together then add to the pan. Mix together well and be sure that all the ingredients are evenly spaced in the pan.

**Bring** to the boil then add the diced tomatoes. Do not mix them into the pan, rather leave them on top of the ingredients.

**Add** the mussels and clams. Don't mix them in, just push them into the stock very slightly.

**Place** the pan on top of a sheet pan so it's easier to move around then put both into a preheated **350 F°** oven. Cook for approximately 35 minutes or until the rice is done.

**Leave** to rest for 10 minutes in a warm place and then serve.

**Serves 8-10**

# SNAPPER MONTE CARLO

## INGREDIENTS

4 (6 oz) red snapper fillets
1 tbsp olive oil
½ cup butter, divided
8 (16-20) shrimp, peeled and deveined
8 large scallops
2 cups Butter Sauce (see recipe page 131)

## METHOD

**In** a sauté pan, heat the olive oil and ¼ cup butter over a moderate heat. Place the fish skin-side down in the pan and cook for approximately 4-5 minutes until slightly brown. Turn the fish over and cook for another 4 minutes. Test the snapper fillets for doneness as all fillets vary in thickness. When cooked, take the fillets out of the pan, cover with foil and put to one side to keep warm.

**Place** the pan back on the stove on a moderate heat and add the last ¼ cup butter and a touch more olive oil. Once heated, place the shrimp and scallops into the pan and cook for 3 minutes on each side.

**Assemble** 4 plates and place a fillet of snapper skin-side up, 2 shrimp and 2 scallops on each plate. Drizzle each plate with 2 tbsp Butter Sauce over the fish and serve.

**Serves 4.**

*Any similar white fish may be substituted for red snapper.*

*At the restaurant we do not skin the fillets of snapper. We season and cook them crisp in the pan. Fresh snapper is widely available in Cayman. I tend to use the large fish fillets as we cook the smaller snapper whole.*

*The Butter Sauce is very extreme and rich so only use a little amount and put the rest in a sauce boat on the table. Personally, I am very fond of this sauce.*

# Halcyon Cove
## Antigua, BVI

After three wonderful years at the Prospect Reef Resort in Tortola I felt it was time to move on. Luckily for me, Mervyn Poulter, a former manager at the Reef, had moved to Antigua a year earlier where he became the general manager at the Halcyon Cove.

The first thing I remember is that the hotel was a lot larger than the Reef. The restaurant was set atop an immense hill with a gorgeous view of Dickenson Bay, and hotel guests were shuttled up via a monorail. Unlike today, I didn't need to visit the fitness centre, as I used to walk to my office and the main kitchen several times a day. Oh, to be young again!

A second restaurant called The Warri Pier was set just off the shore, a fair distance from the hotel. But as the main storeroom was at the restaurant up the hill, you can imagine what fun it was to urgently need some supplies or ingredients!

After a year they built a new restaurant, bar and casino at the ground level of the hotel so my hill climbing days were over. It was a bit of a shame, though, as I'll never forget the spectacular view that was lost when the main restaurant closed. On the plus side, the kitchen in the new building was very modern and much easier to operate.

I was given a lovely house to live in not far from the hotel at the top of the hill overlooking Dickenson Bay. One memorable annual event was racing week when a huge flotilla would sail completely around the island. It was an amazing sight from my house when they landed in our bay, but then they all had to be fed! The boat captains all ate in the main restaurant while the crews enjoyed barbecue on the beach. It was a frantic day, but not too bad as they were soon back out on the water racing to the next location.

Antigua was a fantastic island and I also had the privilege to be there for their independence celebration as they had been a UK protectorate. Princess Margaret represented the Queen and there was a huge party with a 21-gun salute from the Royal Navy. Then they had a ceremony including the raising of the Antiguan Flag and lowering of the Union Jack. It was a great show with an accompanying carnival for two days. I'm embarrassed to say I didn't see the kitchen staff a great deal as it was strictly buffets for all the guests during that time. I only hope they enjoyed the once-in-a-lifetime event as much as I did.

I was in Antigua for, again, three years and I had some very good laughs. I lived with some very big, hairy spiders and a mongoose. It was all an experience...

# SPINACH & FETA TART

## INGREDIENTS

Savoury Pastry (see recipe page 142)
1 lb fresh spinach
4 large eggs
2 cups heavy cream
4 oz feta cheese
4 oz Parmesan cheese, grated
10"x 2¼" deep tart tin, preferably with a loose base

## METHOD

**Preheat** oven to **350°F** and grease the tart tin.
**Roll** the pastry into a circle and carefully place into the tart tin. Cover the pastry with parchment paper and place baking beans in the middle of the pastry to weigh it down. This method is called Baking Blind. Place the tart tin in the oven and cook for approximately 10-15 minutes. Remove the baking beans and parchment paper then leave the pastry to cool for 5 minutes. Adjust the oven to **300°F.**
**Cook** the spinach by plunging it into boiling water, then strain it and leave to the side.
**Mix** the eggs and heavy cream together and mix well.
**Assemble** the tart:
- spread the spinach on the bottom of the tart
- crumble the feta cheese over the spinach
- add the grated Parmesan cheese
- pour the eggs and cream over the top
- using a fork, lightly mix everything together and place the tart on a baking sheet in the oven for approximately 35 minutes. If the tart is getting too brown on the top, cover with tin foil.
**This** tart is best served barely warm so it is good to let it rest for at least 30 minutes before serving.
**Serves 4.**

*Baking beans, on top of parchment paper, are placed onto the pastry to stop it from rising while cooking. There are many materials you can use as baking beans such as dried beans or dried pasta or you can purchase a box of metal or clay beans.*

*It is better to use fresh Parmesan and grate it yourself. Pre-grated Parmesan cheese should not be used.*

*When I first opened Calypso Grill, this was the only tart that would sell. One day a server came to me and said, "This is not a daily tart so why don't we call it the Millennium Tart?" So true.*

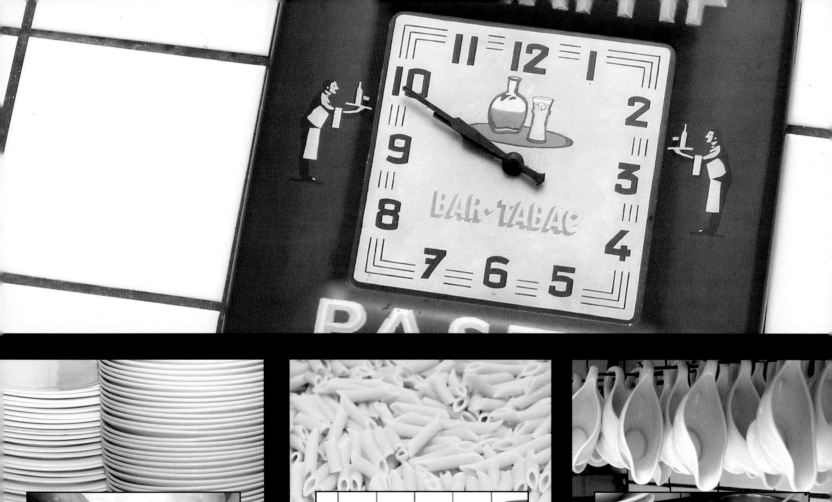

# WAHOO ESCOVEITCH

This is an old Caymanian dish which I modified for the restaurant. It has been on the menu since we opened back in 1999.

## INGREDIENTS

1½ lb fresh fish (wahoo, mahimahi, grouper, snapper)
1 cup Frank's RedHot Original Cayenne Pepper Sauce
2 lb onions, sliced
1 small red pepper, diced small
1 Scotch Bonnet pepper, seeded and chopped fine
1 cup white vinegar
½ cup sugar
Oil for frying (soya bean or corn)
2 cups corn starch

## METHOD

**Cut** the fish into 1-inch cubes. Combine with Frank's RedHot sauce, cover and refrigerate until ready to use.
**In** a saucepan, place the sliced onions, red pepper, Scotch Bonnet pepper, vinegar and sugar. Bring to the boil and cook for approximately 4 minutes, just until the onions are blanched. Remove from heat and leave to the side.
**Prepare** a fryer or put soya bean or corn oil (approximately 3-inches) in a Dutch oven. Heat the oil over a moderate heat and check the temperature by putting a piece of bread in the oil – it should start browning slowly.
**Take** the fish out of the marinade and strain any excess sauce. Coat each piece of fish with the corn starch and then place the pieces into a small sieve and shake off the excess corn starch.
**Place** each piece of fish carefully into your pan or fryer and cook for approximately 5 minutes. Remove from the pan and place the pieces of fish onto paper towel to remove any excess oil.
**Divide** the fish equally onto 4 plates and with a slotted spoon, place the onions over the fish with a little bit of the juice. Serve.
**Serves 4.**

*When cooking the fish, you may want to take a piece out and test to see if it is cooked. You don't want to overcook the fish and please remember that the fish continues to cook after you take it out of the fryer.*

*When cooking the onions, remember not to overcook them as they need to be firm to the touch so they still have a bit of crunch. The onions are spicy in this dish, but if you prefer it not to be too hot, take the seeds out of the Scotch Bonnet pepper before finely chopping.*

*The right frying temperature is 350°F. You can purchase a cooking thermometer to check the temperature.*

# Americana Hotel

## Ocho Rios, Jamaica

My next port of call was Ocho Rios, Jamaica, to one of the first "tower block" high rise hotels on the beach, the Americana. When I first arrived I was quite surprised that they even built hotels like that in the Caribbean but it actually suited the area and was a great hotel.

To be honest, I was a little dubious about working in Jamaica as I had heard that the people were difficult to work with. Well, it turned out to be the exact opposite as they were amongst the best and kindest staff I have ever had. Not only were they hard workers but once they got to know you they were extremely easy going and great fun to be around.

One of the first hurdles I had to jump was that every time I left the hotel to go to town I was stopped continually and asked to check out all the wares people were selling. I mentioned this to my second chef and he walked me down the road and introduced me to all the vendors as the chef of the Americana. I wasn't bothered again and it made my journey into town a lot easier.

When it came to buying fresh produce there was nothing bought overseas — we purchased everything locally as every day the farmers brought their goods directly to us in big trucks. Using large boxes and sacks, they would pour everything out onto canvas so we could see if anything wasn't up to standard. But because the supply was so plentiful, and as the competition amongst farmers increased, the goods were always top quality. When a farmer brought watermelons to the dock they were all marked with his name so if anything was spoiled they were told the following week to replace the bad fruit. It was tough for them but that was the rule. From a chef's view it was heaven working with such fresh organic produce and I'm sure it's the same to this day.

The Jamaican people have their own cuisine and national dishes and jerk pork is one of them. Each day we set up the grill with wonderfully scented pimento wood. A half pig was first marinated in the fridge in a large tin bath after which the chefs would cut it into large joints to cook on the wood. It was fabulous! The truth is, only Jamaicans really know how to cook jerk pork and chicken so I considered myself completely spoilt. They kept the spice fairly mild for the hotel guests but if you ate in town you had to be prepared for some serious heat. I quickly learned that the hard dough bread accompaniment came in very handy to counteract the heavy spice.

One day I was sitting in my office and the boys walked past with a live goat that was bleating. The second chef

told me they were making goat water for our sister hotel's staff party. After they had prepared the goat and had it cooking in a very large pot, I had a look to see what it was like and the top of the goat's head was floating on top. It almost looked as if they had scalped the goat and put it into the pot. They told me it made it taste really good – I took their word for it as I did not try it.

One of my absolute favourite foods is Jamaican beef patties. To illustrate, I recently visited Jamaica to attend the wedding of a good friend. After settling in on my first day I asked the hotel maid if she could please bring me some local beef patties each day on her way to work — that's how much I love them! You can also get them at my current home in Grand Cayman and they are equally good but I can't let it become a habit as, for someone my size, it can be too much of a good thing.

I am really impressed with the local food in Jamaica even to this day. Food is an extremely important part of their culture and it shows in the quality of their cuisine. I think my final word on the subject, and one of the most enjoyable parts of my stay, was drinking Blue Mountain coffee every morning. When I finally left for my next adventure, I really missed that divine treat.

# Delicious Desserts

Sticky Toffee Pudding — 8"

Chocolate Bread Pudding — 8"

Strawberry & Rhubarb Crumble — 8"

Millionaire Shortbread w/Vanilla Icecream — 8"

# Delicious Desserts

Sticky Toffee Pudding — 8"

Chocolate Bread Pudding — 8"

Crumble — 8"

Icecream — 8"

# BAILEYS CRÈME BRÛLÉE

## INGREDIENTS

8 egg yolks
½ cup refined sugar
2 cups heavy cream
½ cup Baileys Irish Cream liqueur
½ cup powdered sugar

## METHOD

**Stir** the egg yolks and refined sugar in a bowl. Bring the cream and the Baileys to the boil then stir into the egg mixture. Place the bowl onto a pot half full of simmering water, making sure the bowl doesn't touch the water. Continue stirring until the custard begins to thicken slightly and has a heavy cream consistency.
**Divide** the custard between six 3-inch ramekin dishes. Sit the ramekins into a roasting pan then pour boiling water into the pan until it comes halfway up the sides of the ramekins. Place into a **210°F** oven for about 20 minutes. **To** check for doneness, take one out and give it a gentle shake to see if it has set. If it's still like liquid put it back into the oven for about 5 minutes more until there is just a slight movement on the surface. Refrigerate overnight.
**Finish** the Crème Brûlées by using a small sieve to sprinkle the powdered sugar liberally over the tops. If you have a blow torch you will achieve a great glaze. If not, place the ramekins under a very hot broiler as close as possible so the sugar will melt and turn brown. If this is not working for you remove from the broiler and just add more sugar on the top. It's best to keep a watchful eye at this stage.
**Usually** I like to place some berries around the plate to serve.
**Serves 6.**

*Be very careful when making this dish as it could curdle if the egg mixture gets too hot. The custard should appear to be very smooth and silky when you pour into the ramekins.*

*And be watchful when you bake them. Keep checking in the oven and give one a little wobble to see how they are getting on. Keep in mind they will set as they cool.*

*I do not use vanilla in this recipe because the Baileys already makes it very sweet.*

*A kitchen blow torch is a worthwhile investment.*

# CHOCOLATE BREAD PUDDING

## INGREDIENTS

8 oz chocolate, semi-sweet
¾ cup sugar, white
2 cups heavy cream
½ cup butter (1 stick)
½ cup Myers rum
½ cup Kahlua
3 eggs, whisked
1 loaf of sliced white bread, crusts removed, quartered

## METHOD

**Place** the chocolate, sugar, heavy cream and butter into a large mixing bowl. Add the Myers rum and Kahlua. Put the mixing bowl on top of a large pan of simmering water, making sure that the bottom of the bowl doesn't touch the water. Stir until melted. Remove from the heat and add the whisked eggs. Mix well.

**Butter** a 7"x11" (2 quart) pudding dish and spread a quarter of the chocolate mixture into the bottom.

**Cover** the chocolate with a layer of bread then pour another quarter of the mix on top. Press the chocolate into the bread with the back of a fork. Continue to do this method twice until you have three layers of bread. Cover with cling film and place into the fridge overnight.

**Place** the pudding dish inside a roasting pan and pour water into the roasting pan to come a third of the way up the pudding dish. Cook for 40 minutes at **350°F** and you will find it comes up like a soufflé. Test the pudding for doneness by lightly touching the top — it should feel spongy to touch.

**Serve** right away, piping hot with cream.

**Serves 6**

*Use a good quality, semi-sweet chocolate.*

*This dish is at its best if you leave it in the fridge overnight to let the bread soak up the chocolate and alcohol.*

*Use a fork to press the bread into the chocolate — make sure there is no white bread showing.*

# Divi Divi Hotel
## Aruba, Dutch Antilles

The next chapter of my career in the Caribbean was in the beautiful Dutch colony of Aruba. Although I hadn't heard much about the island, I was thrilled to get the opportunity to work there.

There were two Divi hotels on Aruba — the Divi Divi where I worked and a sister hotel called Tamarind. Unlike my last experience in Jamaica, the Divi Divi was only two stories high.

The motto of the hotel was barefoot elegance, so the guests didn't have to wear shoes or jackets. And it followed that the Red Parrot dining room was very casual and during the season, very busy indeed. Our specialty was Venezuelan Red Snapper which we bought by the truckload every week from the dock. And as Venezuela was just a hop, skip and a jump across the water the fish were very fresh.

Even though the hotel was casual and laid-back, my work was anything but. I was even expected to greet guests in the lobby if there was a large arrival. And I often received special requests first hand as all department heads were required to provide personal service. I also had to work breakfasts in case there was a special request for dinner. If someone had an allergy, for example, I would make sure it was noted for the evening service.

We were also encouraged to do an activity with the guests once a week. Mine was "Cooking under the Sun with Chef George". I often demonstrated how to cook Calypso Shrimp at poolside and the ladies would all have a sample afterwards. It was a great success and became so popular that the chefs in the kitchen started cooking the shrimp for me so I only had to demonstrate the final preparation.

Everyone would find out when the events were scheduled the night before when a paper was sent to each room called the Blakey Blakey which means news or gossip in Papiamento — the local dialect. The locals also spoke Dutch, English and Spanish.

Twice a year they had week-long shareholder meetings at the hotel which I must admit made me a bit nervous. But after the first year when they got to know me better, as my usual genial self, they were like putty in my hands! Luckily, the owner of the company was also one of my fans so that helped a lot. I'll tell a few more shareholder stories later as I opened a Divi Hotel in the Bahamas in my next adventure.

The name of the company — Divi — comes from a common tree in Aruba of the same name. The constant trade winds from the northeast make the tops of the Divi trees

always point in a south westerly direction and give them their unique appearance. Aruba is a very dry island with not much rain at all (the national plant or flower is Aloe).

Looking back I can honestly say I truly enjoyed my stay in Aruba. The people were wonderful and the hotel very accommodating. Near the end of my stay they built a new building beside the hotel with a large casino called The Alhambra. This preceded a number of other changes and I'm sure I wouldn't recognize Aruba today. But I guess that's progress — I am sure it's still a great place and look forward to visiting there in the near future.

Thursday, December 18, 1986

## Chef George of Divi Divi is big on long lunches

Depicted above is Divi Divi Red Parrot Restaurant Chef George wearing a captioned apron which poses an intriguing point. George, who studied at a culinary arts academy in his native England for seven years, was about to take a chef's position in Buckingham Palace when the Caribbean lured him away instead. Friends say he has eight years in the islands, loves Aruba and Amstel Beer, and is crazy for long, festive luncheons. George holds "Cooking Under the Sun" courses Thursdays at Divi Divi Beach Hotel. This week: Caribbean Shrimp Dumas and Cherries Jubilee, and NEWS readers are invited to audit the course if only to taste the results.

# LEMON TART

## INGREDIENTS

1 quantity of Sweet Pastry (see recipe page 143)
8 egg yolks
2 cups refined sugar
1½ cups heavy cream
4 lemons (finely grated zest from 2, juice from all)
10"x 2¼" deep tart tin, preferably with a loose base

## METHOD

**Preheat** oven to **350°F** and grease the tart tin.
**Roll** the pastry into a circle and carefully place into the tart tin. Cover the pastry with parchment paper and place baking beans in the middle of the pastry to weigh it down. This method is called Baking Blind. Place the tart tin in the oven and cook for approximately 10-15 minutes. Remove the baking beans and parchment paper then leave the pastry to cool for 5 minutes. Adjust the oven to **250°F.**
**Mix** the egg yolks and sugar until dissolved and smooth. Stir in the heavy cream, lemon juice and lemon zest. Pour mixture into the cooled tart shell and bake for 30-35 minutes at **250°F**. Remove from the oven and allow to cool 30-60 minutes.
**Serve** with a nice pour of double cream or heavy cream, slightly whipped, over the top.
**Serves 8.**

*Baking beans, on top of parchment paper, are placed onto the pastry to stop it from rising while cooking. There are many materials you can use as baking beans such as dried beans or dried pasta or you can purchase a box of metal or clay beans.*

*To test the tart for doneness, give the tray a slight shake to see how the filling moves. It should not be liquid but still jiggly as the tart will continue to set while it cools.*

*To serve the tart you can sprinkle it with powdered sugar through a fine sieve to make it look scrumptious.*

# MANGO CREPES

## INGREDIENTS

2 eggs
2 cups whole milk
1½ cups all purpose flour
1 pinch salt
¼ cup unsalted butter, melted
Vegetable oil or Pam spray for greasing the pan
3 large mangoes

## METHOD

- Crepes:

**Whisk** the eggs and milk in a bowl and add the flour and salt, mixing well. Add the melted butter and whisk together.
**Lightly** oil a 6-inch frying pan and heat on medium. When hot, pour enough of the mixture to coat the bottom of the pan very thinly. Cook for approximately 1 minute and flip over to the other side for a further minute.

- Filling:

**Peel** the mangoes and cut the flesh from the stone. Dice the flesh from 2 of the mangoes into a ¼-inch dice and place into a pot.
**Blend** the flesh from the third mango in a blender and then mix with the diced mango. Warm the mixture slightly before assembling the crepe.

- Assemble:

**Place** the crepe onto a plate. Place a tablespoon of the mango mixture down the middle of the crepe and fold in the sides. Serve warm with ice cream.
**Serves 4.**

*There is a saying from chefs about crepes when they are being made: "I want to be able to read the newspaper through them." In other words, keep them very thin.*

*You need to make 4 crepes for this recipe, but continue to make crepes until the batter is finished, as they will keep, wrapped in plastic, in the fridge for weeks. These crepes are great even with just sugar and lemon.*

*At the restaurant we serve Mango Crepes with coconut-pineapple ice cream. You can also spoon a little of the mango mixture onto the top of the folded crepe before serving.*

*With the mango, coconut and pineapple flavours going on it's a very popular dessert for the Caribbean.*

# South Ocean Divi Hotel

## Nassau, Bahamas

This latest move to the Bahamas was also with the Divi group as they renovated a hotel in Nassau and asked if I would open it.

The hotel was still under renovation when I arrived and I had to interview staff, write menus and equip the kitchen. All staff had to be locals according to the law, and work permits were reviewed by the accountant, the manager and of course myself, the chef.

The second chef, being Bahamian, had worked in all the large hotels on Cable Beach and was an enormous help to me. We organized a schedule to interview the prospective staff and to our dismay there were very few with hotel kitchen experience. So I decided to interview all the candidates again and choose the people who were the friendliest and most enthusiastic. Then I taught them all how to work the way I wanted and it turned out great.

We opened with two restaurants — one in the main hotel and an Italian-themed restaurant called Papagallo on the 18th hole of the hotel golf course. After just a few weeks of training we had a soft opening and then the grand opening the following week.

The opening was a lavish affair which included the Prime Minister of the Bahamas to officially open the hotel. We had a buffet around the pool area and all the food was set up in what looked like market stalls. Vegetables and salads in one, a fish stall, meat stall, dairy products, cheese and more — it was a lot of work but looked fantastic. Oh, I almost forgot, we had a great pastry chef and when he wheeled his incredible cart of desserts to the pool area he got a huge round of applause from all the guests.

As if that wasn't enough, just four days later we had a party for the shareholders and the pressure was on to create something memorable. After much deliberation, we decided to take them on an evening bus tour of the island, in the dark. Meanwhile, we secretly made preparations throughout the day and to their surprise, served dinner at the end of the tour on the 13th hole of the golf course. It had to be unusual and, I must say, it was spectacularly so.

For example, we served Marinated Conch as an appetizer. But for added effect, I had the pastry chef cook dough over a bowl with the point of a conch shell as a handle to create a dome. We served this over the salad and put them on the tables just before the guests arrived.

The main course was served from stations as the 13th hole was miles away from the kitchens. I made Beef Wellington which was carved at the last moment and placed on the plate fresh. We also had heating cabinets at each station but with no electricity or sterno heaters for chafing dishes it was certainly a challenge! At one point during our preparations I saw flames coming out of the bottom of a heating cabinet! Luckily, it was only a tray of bread and not a Wellington or I would have thrown a fit.

Meanwhile, all the guests were on the tour bus, not knowing what was going on. The bus took them to the golf course using the back road so they didn't know where they were going. It all looked spectacular when they arrived, with tiki torches and lamps lighting up the 13th hole and even a string quartet playing in the greenside bunker.

When the main course was over, there was another surprise. A gospel choir came over a small hill singing all the way and then gave a beautiful concert for everyone.

This was followed by flaming Baked Alaska for dessert with the staff carrying them ablaze to the tables.

I know the shareholders were really pleased as the president of the hotel came over to me and said that after tonight's show they were going to call me St George!

Whilst in the Bahamas I was also involved with the Bahamas Culinary Association. One night they held a culinary show in a large hotel on Cable Beach judged by six master chefs from the U.S. and all members had to help keep the judges happy during their visit. So I got them playing golf at the hotel and to my horror they asked me to entertain them for dinner at Papagallo restaurant. I was so visibly nervous the staff became more concerned about me than the guests! I told them no food was to go to the table without passing me first. At the end of the evening everything went well but my nerves were definitely tested.

All in all it was a great three years with plenty of stories to tell, but this is a cookbook after all, so let's get back to the recipes.

# MILLIONAIRE SHORTBREAD

## INGREDIENTS

2¾ cups all purpose flour
1¼ cup butter, divided (+ enough to grease tray)
½ cup refined sugar
3 tbsp golden syrup
2 14-oz tins sweetened condensed milk
½ lb chocolate, semi-sweet
2 tbsp heavy cream
1 baking tray (6"x12"x1")

## METHOD

- Shortbread
**Mix** the flour, butter and sugar in a bowl until it forms a dough. Butter the baking tray and place the dough in the centre. Starting from the centre, flatten the dough until it evenly coats the bottom of the tray. Prick the shortbread with a fork.

**Bake** in a **350°F** oven for 10-15 minutes but do not let it get too brown. Remove from oven and cool.

- Caramel
**Place** the golden syrup, condensed milk and ¼ cup butter in a pot. Over a medium heat, stir all the time with a wooden spoon until it thickens slightly and turns a caramel colour. This may take about 15 minutes.
**Remove** from heat, pour the mixture over the shortbread. Spread evenly then leave it to cool.

- Chocolate
**In** a bowl, break the chocolate into small pieces. Add the cream. Place the bowl over a pot half filled with simmering water making sure the bottom of the bowl does not touch the water. Stir until all is mixed and melted.
**Remove** from heat, pour the chocolate over the caramel and again spread evenly. Place into the fridge to cool and set.
**When** cold, loosen the shortbread from the tin and cut the millionaire shortbread into the size of piece you prefer.

*At the restaurant we make individual tart tins but the method I have put in this book is as we make it at home.*

*In the restaurant I use semi-sweet chocolate but at home I use Cadbury Dairy Milk chocolate. The semi-sweet is less sweet but we have loved Cadbury since we were kids!*

*We ate it as a cookie at home in England but in the restaurant we warm it slightly and serve it with vanilla ice cream as a dessert.*

*This is a no-calorie dessert, ha ha!*

# NEW YORK CHEESE CAKE

1 lb plain pound cake
¾ cup refined sugar
3 tsp corn starch
1½ lb cream cheese
2 eggs
1 tsp vanilla extract
2 cups whipping cream (40% fat cream)
10-inch spring form cake pan

**Preheat** oven to **350°F.** Butter or spray the cake tin.

**Cut** the pound cake into horizontal slices ¼-inch thick. Cut the slices to fit the bottom of the cake tin until it is covered.

**Mix** the sugar and cornstarch in a mixing bowl and then beat the cream cheese into the mixture until it has a creamy texture.

**Beat** in the eggs slowly and the vanilla extract. Slowly add the cream, beating constantly, until it is a thick and creamy consistency. Pour the mixture onto the pound cake base and smooth over the top.

**Sit** the tin in a baking pan with warm water about ½-inch deep. Place in the oven and bake for 45-50 minutes or until the cheesecake is set and a golden brown colour. Remove from the oven and leave it to cool.

**Take** the cake out of the tin and it's ready to serve.

**Serves 8.**

*Slowly beat the eggs, and also the cream, into the mixture. It will turn out lighter.*

*When cooking, check the cake and if not quite cooked, leave it in the oven, but check every 5-10 minutes.*

*I prefer to eat cheesecake at room temperature – before refrigeration it has a nice creamy texture.*

# La Belle Creole

## St Martin, French West Indies

After many years with Divi hotels I felt it was time to move again. This time I went to St Martin — a gorgeous island separated into French and Dutch territories. The capital of the Dutch side is Philipsburg and the French capital is Marigot, giving the island a bit of a split personality.

The La Belle Creole Hotel was one of the most beautiful I have ever worked in with its peninsular setting and private beach. Its appearance was like a quaint village in Provence with stone stairways leading up to the rooms antd a cobblestone courtyard and central fountain. The reception area included the entrance to the main restaurant and I was most pleased with the overall layout.

I lived in an apartment immediately above the reception area. The room had beautiful French windows and a Romeo and Juliet balcony overlooking the square. On my days off I would load up my old beat-up jeep with supplies (mainly beer) and go to one of the many beautiful beaches to party. Being on the French side, I have to admit we visited a number of the nude beaches as well, but did not participate!

Orient Beach had a hut where they used to make the best barbecued ribs I have ever tasted — so that was a popular visit at least once a week. Many of the locals put barbecue grills near the beaches and in the evening we often visited them for local lobster and fresh fish. Very simple but sooo delicious!

One of my other favourite eating places was a small restaurant called Cha-Cha-Cha. It had similar Caribbean colours to Calypso Grill in Grand Cayman (my current restaurant) and I especially enjoyed the funky bar with jars of rum-soaked fruit which they used to make different flavoured drinks. The menu was tapas so we used to order a variety of foods to accompany the rum. Oh, how fun it was to be young!

The hotel was managed by the Conrad Hilton Hotel Group with owners from the Paribas Bank in Paris. One evening the big bosses came to the hotel and asked me to go to dinner. The best French restaurants were in a village named Grand Cass outside of Marigot. There was a lot of great food on the French side of the island as they had regular containers coming from France — many were as good as anything found in Paris.

On the menu that night was fresh foie gras and the main boss ordered a bottle of Sauternes wine to go with it. But, as I was the only person at the table eating foie gras, I thought it was a bit extreme to order a whole bottle however one doesn't argue with the boss and apparently, that's how it's done in France. Regardless, the waiters were asked to remove the bottle as soon as I had finished the dish, even though I only drank half a glass of the wine!

One of the great treats of living in St Martin was you could take a 20-minute ferry ride to the British Overseas Territory of Anguilla. My favourite place on the island was Cap Juluca which was a posh resort frequented by plenty of movie stars and other famous people. Luckily for us the manager gave us permission to use their beach and other facilities and we often had lunch at their beach-side restaurant, Pimms. Amidst flowing curtains and elegant table settings I enjoyed my favourite: Lobster Club Sandwich. When you ordered it they would pull a lobster out of the catch and cook it for you fresh. Fantastic!

Whilst I was there Queen Elizabeth II visited the island and also had lunch at Pimms and of course it was closed to the public. Shortly thereafter I asked one of the waiters if he knew which chair the Queen had sat on and that's exactly where I had my lunch that day — on the very same chair.

Believe it or not I actually did do some work at the hotel during my time there. Unfortunately, however, I did not greatly improve my French language skills. Most of the cooks spoke French and Creole but the boys who were local to the island only learned French at school and their first language was English. This was lucky for me but did not help my French at all. It didn't matter in the long run, though, as my next calling was to go to Moscow, Russia.

# RHUBARB & STRAWBERRY CRUMBLE

This is a very basic crumble recipe. It's how my mother made it at home. It seems to be very popular at the restaurant.

## INGREDIENTS

1½ lb fresh rhubarb, cut into 1-inch pieces (or 1 lb frozen)
1 cup sugar for the rhubarb
1 cup sugar for the crumble
¼ cup unsalted butter for the rhubarb
¾ cup unsalted cold butter for the crumble
2 cups all purpose flour
2 cups strawberries, stemmed and halved

## METHOD

**Place** the rhubarb into a pan with 4 tbsp water - just enough to cover the bottom of the pan. Stir in the sugar and butter and bring to the boil then remove from the heat, cover, and leave for approximately 10 minutes.

**To** make the crumble, mix the sugar, cold butter and flour in a bowl. Rub together with your fingers until crumbly.

**Place** the rhubarb mixture into a buttered 3-pint pudding dish and place the strawberries on top. Layer the crumble on top of the fruit, sprinkle a little sugar on top and bake at **425°F** for 15-20 minutes or until golden brown.

**Serve** hot with ice cream or heavy cream – whatever takes your fancy.

**Serves 6.**

When cooking the rhubarb use only 4 tbsp water. This is to prevent the rhubarb from sticking. The rhubarb will make its own syrup when cooked.

To make the crumble, use cold butter. Cut the butter into small pieces to make it easier to form the crumbs. Having cold hands also helps.

Always keep an eye on desserts while they're baking.

There are a variety of fruits you can use. Apples are a favourite. Cook the apples the same way as the rhubarb. It prevents them from breaking up too much.

When I first put this dish on the menu I only used rhubarb and it did not sell well until somebody on this side of the world told me they didn't recognize rhubarb unless it's mingled with strawberries. So I did and it was a success, strangely enough.

I always use chopped dates instead of whole ones. They dissolve much better in the water. I also believe they make the cake mixture lighter.

When making the cake mixture, be sure to beat the sugar and butter well until fluffy. And when adding the dates to the bowl mixture, don't over mix.

The Sticky Sauce is everybody's favourite and they normally ask for more so I suggest you double the recipe and everyone will love you. I have to say this has been one of our signature dishes of Calypso Grill. We serve a lot every day.

# STICKY TOFFEE PUDDING

## INGREDIENTS

**Pudding**

2 cups pitted dates, chopped
1 cup water
½ cup unsalted butter
1½ cups refined sugar
4 large eggs, beaten
2 tsp baking soda
2¼ cups all purpose flour

## METHOD

**Grease** an 11"x 7" baking tin.
**Boil** the dates in the water for 2 minutes once they have come to the boil.
**Cream** the butter and refined sugar together in a bowl until fluffy. Add the beaten eggs slowly until well mixed. Add the flour and baking soda to the butter-sugar bowl but do not mix.
**Pour** the dates atop the flour in the bowl. Mix together quickly and pour into your prepared baking tin.
Bake at **350°F** for 30-40 minutes or until it feels just firm to the touch.

## INGREDIENTS

**Sticky Sauce**

2 cups heavy cream
1 cup dark brown sugar
1 tsp cornstarch (optional)

## METHOD

**Place** heavy cream and brown sugar into a pot and stir over low heat until it comes to the boil. Continue stirring over low heat and simmer for about 10 minutes so that it slightly thickens. If desired, mix cornstarch in a little water then stir into the sauce for a slightly thicker sauce.
**To serve,** portion the warm pudding onto plates and top with the hot Sticky Sauce. Accompany with heavy cream and/or ice cream.
**Serves 6-8.**

# Palace Hotel

## Moscow, Russia

I believe this was the bravest move I ever made as I had no idea what I was letting myself in for. I secured a one year contract with the Palace Hotel in Moscow and, in spite of all the challenges, I wouldn't have missed it for the world.

Working in Russia after ten years of Caribbean sunshine in resort-style hotels was a very different experience, to say the least. In a city centre hotel you are catering more towards business people while in resort hotels people are usually on vacation and are therefore much easier to please.

Simply arriving in Moscow was a drama in itself. My plane was delayed leaving Paris and so it was very late at night when I arrived. Nobody from the hotel met me and my first lesson was that taxis didn't exist. Instead, there was a ragtag group of privately owned vehicles and you negotiated a price for the ride. So I reluctantly got in to a car, which was a real banger, and after packing in all my bags the driver couldn't even get it started. I got quite nervous about then but he finally got the car going and we lurched off. He kept saying something about McDonalds which was the only word I understood. Later I learned he was telling me they had the biggest McDonalds restaurant in the world and were quite proud of it! I was so relieved when we finally made it to the hotel in one piece.

Until my arrival I was quite unaware of the political turmoil at that time in Russia. Boris Yeltsin was about to become the leader of the country and it was not an easy transition. There were many public demonstrations including some at the underground train stations. Shortly thereafter I was watching CNN in my apartment and saw that there was a coup underway in the city. So instead of taking the train, which would have been quite risky, my employer sent a car for me and I ended up staying at the hotel for a week until things settled down.

Business at the hotel went on as usual even as I sat in my office listening to gunshots in the streets outside. It was a real war zone and we kept glued to CNN to see what was happening. Strangely, I didn't feel personally threatened though, as the doors to the hotel were locked and security was very tight at all times.

One night, walking back to the hotel after dinner, I didn't notice that a manhole in the street was uncovered and, being as clumsy as I am, my foot went right into the hole. I had a cashmere fawn coat on and it was black with dirt. What a mess. The crowd I was with kept on walking, not realizing what had happened — they didn't even look back! When I eventually gathered myself together and staggered back to the hotel I found them sitting in the hotel bar drinking cocktails. Needless to say I went a bit crazy but soon all was forgiven and it turned into the joke of the month.

I had some wonderful cultural experiences in Russia and fell in love with the Bolshoi theatre which regularly featured the best operas and ballets. One night as we sat in our private box I had a quick peek inside the larger box next to us. There were plush velvet chairs and I was told it had been the box for the Czars and now for the presidents of Russia. I'll never forget the grandeur of that place.

I lived in Moscow for one year and came to dread the dark, drab, sunless days which were so common. Being surrounded by massive grey buildings with empty shop windows seemed especially sad but I'm sure it's quite different now. In spite of the dreary

atmosphere, when you entered the hotel's front doors it was like walking into Aladdin's cave with the hotel being so modern and bright. The transition from the street was amazing.

All foods for the hotel were imported into Moscow as supplies in the city were extremely scarce. We had a large container from France every week for the fresh produce and meats. The truck would park on the road outside the back of the hotel and I had to watch until everything was safely delivered and secured, otherwise boxes had a tendency to grow legs and run.

The local shopping was quite an experience. Usually our driver bought fresh vegetables and fruits from the market but one day I asked my sous chef to take me. He asked if I was sure and of course I agreed not knowing what I was in for.

The market was absolutely huge and the first thing to hit me was the noise which was deafening. Then we went through a door leading to where the meat was sold and the whole area was a choking blue haze of Russian cigarette smoke. All the meat was cut into joints on the tables but the most amazing counter was the chickens. They were dissected on the spot and each part of the chicken was sold separately. You could even buy a single chicken wing. Although everything was quite sanitary and the produce was good, I found I could hardly breathe and had to leave the area pretty quickly.

They provided a television in my apartment but with

only local Russian stations I had an antenna installed on the roof of the building for outside coverage. But only two days later I couldn't get a signal. So I rang the company to check it out and they informed me the antenna was missing. I told them to put up another and within short order the same thing happened. After two more replacements I finally gave up. Apparently the whole apartment block knew what was going on and I was simply feeding the local economy. So I did without television. It was a bit frustrating at the time but looking back I can now see the funny side of things.

The new Russian president, Boris Yeltsin, came to officially open the hotel when we were more or less up and running. He and his staff had a meeting with the owners of the hotel and he brought his own caviar and vodka to the meeting. So putting two and two together I thought this caviar must be the best in Russia and told the waitress to make sure if there was any leftover it had to go straight to my office. Luckily for me it was barely touched and I sat in my office with fresh blinis (a thin pancake) and tasted the caviar — it was like nectar in my mouth. I don't think I'm ever going to taste caviar like it again in my life. Mind you, if you don't get good caviar from the president of Russia where are you going to get it?

One day, whilst I was working in the kitchen, the manager approached me to say the mayor of Moscow was coming for dinner with his guest, the ambassador of Portugal. After the initial panic wore off, I decided to cook Beef Wellington and carve it in the restaurant for them.

I went ahead with my preparations and brought my translator along in case the mayor wanted to say something to me. The translator was extremely nervous as she told me we would be serving the most powerful man in Moscow which of course set my nerves on edge all over again. Luckily everything came off as planned and the mayor told my translator if it tasted as good as it looked, the meal would be fantastic. With great relief I instructed the pastry chef to do a special dessert and once again, everything appeared to go well.

After the meal the manager came into the kitchen and told me the mayor wanted to see me. The panic set in again and my nervous translator came with me. Imagine our mutual relief to hear the mayor say it was one of the best meals he'd ever had. Then he presented me with a beautiful watch with the mayor's coat of arms on the face. He told me he originally planned to give it to the ambassador, but would present him with another watch the next day. It truly was an amazing honour and I have treasured it ever since.

Looking back on those many cold, dark and dreary Moscow days, that moment made it all worthwhile. When my year's contract was over, I must say that I wasn't sorry, but I wouldn't have missed those Moscow experiences for the world.

# BASIC BROWN SAUCE

## INGREDIENTS

4 celery stalks, roughly chopped
2 large carrots, roughly chopped
1 large onion, roughly chopped
1 bay leaf
1 tbsp vegetable oil
1 tbsp tomato paste
2 tbsp flour
4 cups beef stock

## METHOD

**Place** the vegetables and bay leaf in a Dutch oven or deep sauce pan with the vegetable oil and sauté until the vegetables begin to brown.
**Stir** in the tomato paste and flour and blend well.
**Slowly** add the stock until all the flour and tomato paste forms a sauce. Simmer uncovered over low-medium heat for a further 30 minutes. Stir often to keep from burning. Strain the vegetables out of the sauce.
**Makes 2½ cups.**

*If you have fresh thyme or fresh oregano place them with the vegetables to add flavour (this is optional).*

*If the sauce is not brown enough for your use there are some browning agents on the shelves in the local market. Please use very sparingly as this is a strong colouring product.*

*The beef stock is in boxes in the market grocery section. Some are low sodium so bear in mind they have less flavour.*

*Also, if, in your opinion, the sauce has not much flavour for your taste, add some beef bouillon but use sparingly as this could make your finished sauce salty if over used.*

*The Basic Brown Sauce we make at the restaurant is with veal bones and is a 2-day effort so I have made a much simpler version here. Hope it works for you.*

# BUTTER SAUCE

## INGREDIENTS

1 stick celery, 1-inch dice
2 big tomatoes, 1-inch dice
1 med onion, 1-inch dice
3 stems fresh parsley
¼ cup lime juice
4 cups chicken stock
1 lb cold butter, cut into 1-inch cubes

## METHOD

**Place** the celery, tomatoes, onion and parsley into a pot. Add the lime juice and chicken stock and bring to the boil. Reduce the heat to simmer and reduce the liquid by half. Remove from the heat.

**Take** the cold cubes of butter and, piece by piece, whisk them into the mixture. This part is tricky as you don't want to split the butter.

**When** all is mixed, use a hand blender and blitz the sauce. Strain into a clean pan with a fine mesh strainer and leave, covered, in a warm place by the stove until needed.

**Makes 2 cups**

*Do not put this sauce back onto the heat or the butter will split.*

*Remember when making this sauce to never put it back onto the stove to boil once the stock is reduced. What I suggest is that once the sauce is finished, keep it warm near the stove, but not directly on it.*

*This sauce does not have cream to stabilize it, so if you are not comfortable in making this sauce, I suggest you make the Lemon Butter Sauce as a good substitute.*

*I find this sauce is very easy, but then again, I am experienced enough not to split the sauce. It is good to test your skills as a cook!*

*Used for Snapper Monte Carlo (recipe page 87) and is nice with chicken, fish (grilled, baked, poached) and pasta.*

# CALYPSO HOUSE SALAD DRESSING

## INGREDIENTS

1 small onion, peeled and roughly chopped
1 tbsp salt
¼ cup rice wine vinegar
1 cup olive oil
½ cup soy bean or light vegetable oil

## METHOD

**Place** the onion, salt and rice wine vinegar into a food processor and puree. Slowly add the oils.
**Store** in the fridge until ready to use; stir well before using.
**Makes 2½ cups.**

*Keeps well in the fridge, covered, for a week.*

*Used for Calypso House Salad (recipe page 17).*

# CAPER SAUCE

## INGREDIENTS

¾ cup mayonnaise
¼ cup capers, drained and chopped
½ lime, juiced

## METHOD

**Mix** together the mayonnaise, capers and lime juice.
**Makes 1 cup.**

*The mayonnaise I prefer to use is Hellmann's as I believe it is a good quality.*

*At the restaurant we use this sauce for Crabcakes (recipe page 36), Fish & Chips and our Blackened Fish Sandwich.*

*I prefer using Caper Sauce rather than Tartar Sauce.*

*Caper Sauce can be stored in the fridge for up to 4 weeks.*

# CHIPOTLE SAUCE

## INGREDIENTS

½ chipotle pepper (in adobe sauce), chopped
½ cup white wine
1 cup heavy cream
¼ cup butter cut into ½-inch cubes, kept cold

## METHOD

**Place** the chipotle peppers into a pan with the white wine. Bring to a boil and cook for about 3 minutes.
**Add** the cream and bring back to the boil. Reduce for 5 minutes on high heat.
**Remove** from the heat and slowly whisk in each piece of butter, one at a time. Blitz with a hand blender. Do not boil the sauce after adding the butter.
**Makes 1½ cups.**

*The chipotle peppers are very hot. If you prefer the sauce to be on the milder side, use less chipotle pepper as this recipe is quite hot.*

# CUMBERLAND SAUCE

## INGREDIENTS
1 cup red currant jelly
1 cup port wine
½ cup chicken stock
1 tsp cornstarch
1 tsp cold water

## METHOD
**In** a pot place the redcurrant jelly, port wine and chicken stock. Bring to the boil then simmer for 5 minutes.
**Mix** the cornstarch and cold water together to form a paste. Whisk the cornstarch mixture into the pot and continue to simmer for another 5 minutes.
**Cool** and refrigerate.
**Makes 2 cups.**

*This sauce is a very old recipe from the U.K. It is usually served with cold ham, cold game or a savoury pie. At the restaurant we serve it with the Duck Confit (recipe page 38) and the Chicken Liver Pâté.*

*This sauce will keep for 2-3 weeks in the refrigerator in a screw top jar.*

# LEMON or HERB BUTTER SAUCE

¼ cup butter
2 shallots, finely chopped
1 cup heavy cream
1 cup white wine
Juice of 1 lemon
1 cup fish or chicken stock
Optional: fresh parsley, oregano and basil, finely chopped

**Place** the butter into a pan. Add shallots and sauté until translucent.
**Add** heavy cream, white wine, lemon and stock. Bring to the boil then let simmer to reduce by half. Strain in a fine sieve. Leave to the side until needed. Season to taste.
**Makes 2 cups**

*Add finely chopped fresh parsley, oregano and basil to make **Herb Butter Sauce** for Fish Cakes (recipe page 70).*

*When bringing the sauce up to simmering be careful not to boil the sauce too much otherwise it will boil over and make quite a mess (as we see often in the kitchen).*

*If you are making a chicken dish with the same sauce you add chicken stock instead of fish stock.*

*You will find this recipe good for fish and chicken alike. In the restaurant we serve it with grilled fish and grilled chicken breast.*

# Scotland

## Auld Lang Syne

When I was training with British Transport Hotels in Midland and Manchester all the city hotels were more or less quiet in the summer so the staff were sent to busier places within our company.

One summer I was fortunate enough to be chosen to go to the Old Course Hotel in St Andrews. It was a gorgeous new hotel with all the modern conveniences including a new kitchen and a prep room in the basement with fridges — just like a big larder.

I was working on my own in that area prepping the meat and fish one shift when the chef's voice came over the intercom asking me to bring him something upstairs. But the chef had this strong French accent and I started sweating and panicking like crazy as I had no clue what he was saying. After a few minutes, with me frozen to the spot, the chef repeated his request again and I thought to myself, should I run upstairs and ask him or just pack my bags and leave? So I was extremely relieved when the second chef appeared to see what was going on. I told him I didn't understand what the chef wanted and he explained that was why he had come down to help. I could have kissed his feet!

Lucky for me I got away with that one and when that same second chef later came to the Midland Hotel to work I found him a place to live in Manchester and we became good friends.

The highlight of my season at St Andrews was hosting the Bing Crosby and Bob Hope golf tournament as I was able to occasionally take time off to watch the legends play. Of course they were staying at the hotel and Bob Hope had a table of 10 to 12 people every night. The waiters told me his group was quite rowdy and had lots of fun. I asked if Bing Crosby was also there but they told me he had room service alone every night. We all thought that was a bit strange, but I'm sure he must have been tired of being hounded by all of us fans and decided to just take it easy and play golf. Can you blame him?

When we closed the Holiday Inn in Grand Cayman in 1997 I decided to open my own restaurant in Scotland on the Isle of Bute — one of the most beautiful places I have ever been. The restaurant was at the front part of a Victorian pavilion with windows all along the front of the restaurant and an ocean view all the way to the mainland. The island had a lovely old Victorian home on the seafront which was spectacular to see as you approached.

I had golfing friends in Scotland who came for dinner one evening. As a surprise my partner at the restaurant arranged for a piper as they came off the ferry, and there were also sweet lassies dancing on the pier. One friend still talks about it to this day. Contrary to some people, I love the sound of bagpipes which often bring a tear to my eye at their haunting sound.

Strange to say, but another famous tourist attraction was the Victorian toilets which were just a few yards from the restaurant. They were immaculate and to this day are one of the biggest attractions on the island — well worth a visit if you ever travel there.

In the summer a famous boat called The Waverley would stop at the island and you could go on a day trip through the Kyles for even more breathtakingly beautiful scenery.

One of my favourite restaurants ever is Lock Fyne — a seafood restaurant on the loch itself, famous for its oysters and smoked salmon which they do on the premises, not to mention the fresh mussels and scallops! What more could you ask for?

Just down the road from St Andrews Lord Richard Attenborough had a farm with Highland cattle. He used to come to the restaurant quite often and I remember him as a true gentleman. You could not meet a finer person.

I would probably be on the Isle of Bute today if the winters weren't so cruel. It wasn't the cold in particular, but the sea became so rough there were many days when the ferry was cancelled. Because of that there were not many visitors in the winter and business suffered. So I made the decision to leave beautiful Scotland and open Calypso Grill in Grand Cayman.

# PASTRY
## - SAVOURY -

### INGREDIENTS
2½ cups all purpose flour
A pinch of salt
¾ cup cold unsalted butter, cut into small cubes
Ice cold water

### METHOD
**Mix** the flour and salt together. Add the butter and rub together with your fingers until the mixture looks like the texture of bread crumbs.

**Form** a well in the middle of the flour mixture. Add ice cold water, a bit at a time, and mix briefly to a smooth dough. Wrap the pastry into cling film wrap and refrigerate for 20 minutes.

**Makes 1 10"x 2¼" tart tin.**

*This Savoury Pastry is used for Spinach & Feta Tart (recipe page 90), meat pies, and savoury tarts and pies.*

# PASTRY
## - SWEET -

### INGREDIENTS
2½ cups all purpose flour
1 cup powdered sugar
A pinch of salt
1 cup unsalted butter, cut into small cubes
1 egg
1 tsp milk

### METHOD
**Mix** the flour, sugar and salt together. Add the butter cubes and rub together with your fingers until the mixture looks like the texture of bread crumbs.
**Beat** the egg with the milk.
**Form** a well in the middle of the flour mixture. Pour the egg mixture into the well and mix briefly to a smooth dough. Wrap the pastry into cling film wrap and refrigerate for 20 minutes.
**Makes 1 10"x 2¼" tart tin.**

*This Sweet Pastry is used for the Lemon Tart (recipe page 109) and any type of sweet pies.*

## INGREDIENTS

2 tbsp butter
1 large shallot, small dice
1 cup red wine
2½ cups Basic Brown Sauce (see recipe page 130)

## METHOD

**Place** the butter and shallots into a sauce pan. Sauté on medium heat until translucent.

**Increase** heat to high, add the red wine and boil to reduce by half.

**Add** the Brown Sauce and continue to cook until the sauce thickens and will coat the back of a spoon. At this stage you can strain the sauce but I prefer to keep in the shallots.

**Makes 2½ cups**

*This sauce can be used, as I have, with steaks, chicken (whole, roast or breasts) and also lamb, if you so desire.*

# WHITE WINE BUTTER SAUCE

## INGREDIENTS

2 cups boxed vegetable stock
½ cup white wine
2 sticks celery, 1-inch dice
1 small onion, 1-inch dice
2 plum tomatoes, quartered
4 stems fresh basil
4 stems fresh parsley
½ cup cold butter, 1-inch cubes

## METHOD

**In** a pot, add the vegetable stock and white wine. Add the celery, onion, tomatoes, basil and parsley. Bring to the boil. Skim the top and turn the heat down to simmer until the liquid has reduced by half. Take off the heat and leave to cool slightly – approximately 10 minutes.

**Slowly** whisk butter cubes into the pot. The butter has to be cold for this. Keeping the pot off the heat, whisk in the butter and when melted, use a blender to blend all the ingredients together.

**Using** a fine strainer, strain the above, discarding the vegetables. Leave the sauce in a warm place, but it is very important that this sauce does not go back on the heat as it will split and turn into a right mess!

**Season** to taste and serve.

**Makes 2 cups**

*This is more of a complex sauce to make, but tastes so good it's worth the extra effort!*
*For this sauce, it would be ideal to use an immersion blender, but a regular blender works as well.*
*It is OK to serve sauces for fish dishes at room temperature.*
*This sauce is used for the Snapper Monte Carlo (recipe page 87) and is also nice on pasta...a little rich, but nice.*

# Cayman Islands
## Sticky Toffee Lane

I first came to Grand Cayman to work at the Holiday Inn on Seven Mile Beach some 20 years ago. If there was ever a hotel set in its ways, the Holiday Inn was it. Perhaps this was partly because the majority of the staff were locals which you don't often see these days and they were used to a slower pace of life. I especially remember, with much fondness, the ladies in the kitchen. As an outsider they sometimes gave me a hard time but I knew they really liked me in their own way.

I had known of the Holiday Inn for years from visiting my close friends and business partners at Calypso Grill — James and Terry. So it was no surprise to me that there was a lot of sorrow in 1998 when the old hotel was knocked down to make way for the Ritz-Carlton.

After working at the Holiday Inn I had my beautiful, little venture in Scotland and then went on a three-week vacation to Tokyo while Calypso Grill was being built. When I returned to Grand Cayman the restaurant was ready to go, even though I hadn't ever stepped inside. I clearly remember walking through the front doors that first day as I was immediately struck by the vibrant Caribbean colours and décor. So I'm not surprised today when people walk into the restaurant and I can see they are both amazed and enchanted.

The kitchen, however, was another story. It was extremely small, hot and somewhat ill-equipped, but I somehow figured out how to make do as there was no turning back. Of course we now have the latest refrigeration, equipment and air-conditioning which makes it considerably easier to manage.

It's not easy to start any restaurant but even more so on a small island — if you don't get it right the first time you're going to be in a lot of trouble. However, given how busy we've been since the start I think I can safely say we got it right. Many items on the menu have become signature dishes like the Wahoo Escoveitch, Lobster and Shrimp Champagne, Mango Shrimp, Crabcakes and of course the famous Sticky Toffee Pudding for which this book, and a street nearby, was named. I am proud to say these dishes have been in such consistently high demand that they haven't changed in 15 years.

More often than not customers know what they are going to eat even before they arrive at Calypso Grill. Of course we offer a variety of daily specials that cater to those looking for something different, but I don't dare remove any of our popular items from the menu. I've tried to switch things up before and believe me they let me know and I always want to make sure everyone leaves happy.

One of the advantages of being a chef is you get to meet a few famous people along the way and cook for them if you are really lucky. Here at Calypso we have cooked for President Clinton, Sir Richard Branson, Eric Ripert and Cheryl Crowe to name a few.

In 2005, after construction of the new Ritz-Carlton was completed, Cheryl Crowe was the featured performer at the spectacular gala opening of the hotel. Afterwards, I was delighted to serve her dinner at Calypso and went to her table to recommend the Sticky for dessert. Imagine my surprise when she said it had already been recommended to her! Later as she was leaving she told me that normally she didn't eat desserts but amazed herself by devouring the whole thing. She was truly a lovely person. And another famous singer visited us at a later date — the amazing Alicia Keyes, whose gorgeous voice was only matched by her wonderful personality.

We have a big fan base for the Sticky Toffee Pudding. Stephen Colbert said it was his favourite dessert so his wife even invited me to New York to serve it at his 50th birthday party. I felt so honoured to attend and serve him personally at the table.

We also hosted the great comedian Steve Martin and have cooked for numerous sports celebrities. NBA star, Dirk Nowitzki, came into the kitchen to have his picture taken with all the cooks. Given Dirk's height of seven feet we had to bring chairs into the kitchen to stand on which made a fairly comical photo. He was a great sport about the whole thing and a really nice guy. Andy Pettitte and Jorg Posada of the New York Yankees also visited us one year and of course the staff were in seventh heaven!

The one setback in all my years in Grand Cayman was Hurricane Ivan which devastated the island in September of 2004. Calypso Grill was pretty much destroyed except for one small part of the kitchen. Fortunately I was on vacation in England at the time and missed most of the turmoil. When I finally returned in January 2005 to help with the rebuilding I have to admit I may have been more of a hindrance than a help. One of the jobs I was given was to hold a shield whilst they spray-painted Calypso's window shutters. On one especially breezy afternoon it all went horribly wrong and I ended up bluer than the clear Caribbean sky — even my glasses. I kept a low profile after that and, to everyone's relief, concentrated working inside on the kitchen. After considerable effort, Calypso Grill was put back together as if Ivan had never happened. I can't thank the staff and those who assisted with the construction enough.

Apart from my work at Calypso Grill, I truly love living in the Cayman Islands. And I want to sincerely thank everyone concerned in providing me with the privilege of becoming a Caymanian citizen. I have made a great many friends here who I hold dear. I also have friends who regularly visit Calypso Grill from all parts of the world and I always look forward to seeing them every year.

In closing, I think that it's fitting that my journey down Sticky Toffee Lane concludes in Grand Cayman, as this, I feel, is truly now my home.

# INDEX